100
—YEARS OF—
Classic
STEAM

5013 100 Years of Classic Steam
This edition published in 1997 by CLB
Distributed in the USA by BHB International Inc.,
30 Edison Drive, Wayne, New Jersey 07470
This compilation © 1997 CLB International,
Godalming, Surrey, England
Printed in China
ISBN 1-85833-661-9

100 YEARS OF — Classic STEAM

COLIN GARRATT

CLB

Contents

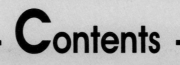

Introduction

It is popularly supposed that the world's first steam locomotive was Stephenson's *Rocket*. In truth, however, the first example appeared exactly a quarter of a century before this in 1804, when Richard Trevithick's engine emerged from a South Wales ironworks. Yet it was with the *Rocket* that certain basic principles were established: it had a multi-flue tube boiler, used exhaust steam to create a draught on the fire, and had a direct drive from the cylinders. In these fundamentals, the steam locomotive was to change little throughout its entire existence, despite the aspirations of innumerable individuals and design teams over subsequent years.

The advent of steam traction enabled industrial development, then in its infancy, to grow and spread with much greater speed than previously. At last, raw materials could be conveyed quickly and efficiently from source to manufacturer and from manufacturer to customer, while ordinary people found they were no longer confined to the small villages and market towns in which they were raised; in short, the social and industrial revolution thus wrought by the age of steam ensures it a fundamental place in world history.

This is not to propagandise for steam as much as for the transport system it created. The steam locomotive does have inherent weaknesses that, arguably, render it unsuitable for conditions in many countries, especially the developed ones. However, forsaking the railways altogether and basing national economies upon road transportation is untenable. The road system demands limitless financial resources in order to sustain it, while constituting a wanton dissipation of energy supplies. Future generations may well regard an overwhelming dependence upon road transport as one of the biggest acts of folly committed during the twentieth century.

During its development, the steam locomotive diversified into tens of thousands of different types. This incredible variety was due to two prime factors: firstly, railway systems large and small the world over invariably wanted their own designs, and secondly, throughout its entire evolution, locomotive designers were under constant pressure to enlarge and improve their products in the face of an unremitting demand for heavier and faster trains.

Another factor that ensured variety was the absence of any agreed international design, such as occurs with aeroplanes and road vehicles and other major forms of transport. Although heavy standardisation was achieved in a few countries, cross fertilisations were few and, when they did occur, were invariably due to war operations or reparation packages following a war. Of course, the private locomotive builders, particularly those specialising in industrial locomotives, had their own ranges of standard designs, but even these were varied to suit the needs (or fantasies) of the recipient. Also remarkable is the fact that few condemned engines were ever sold to other countries. Although international differences in gauge sometimes inhibited such manoeuvres, there were still many instances where such sales might have taken place, but due to constantly changing operating conditions – the very thing that fostered diversity in the first place – such actions were usually rendered inappropriate.

North America produced more locomotives than any other part of the world and it is remarkable that so few builders emerged, especially as the nation's railroads seldom built their own locomotives – a direct contrast with the situation in Britain. Although a wide variety of foundries did emerge during the nineteenth century, the early years of the twentieth century saw the vast majority of the country's locomotives – both for home and export – coming from the works of the big three: Baldwin of Philadelphia, the American Locomotive Company (ALCO) of New York and Montreal, and Lima of Ohio. By far the biggest name was Baldwin, founded by Mathias Baldwin, who produced America's first home-built locomotive in 1832. Over the following one-and-a-quarter centuries, this prodigiously successful company produced some 70,000 locomotives. So successful was Baldwin that other builders banded together to form the American Locomotive Company in an endeavour to compete and into ALCO went such famous nineteenth-century names as Rodgers and Cook, both of Paterson, New Jersey. After the big three came the celebrated industrial builders, the most prolific being H. K. Porter of Pittsburgh, Pennsylvania. But it is the big three, along with their subsidiaries, that represent the core of American production, with the incredible total of some 180,000 locomotives among them, embracing literally thousands of different classes tailored to match the requirements and image of the many railroads for which they built, both at home and overseas.

The largest class of steam locomotive in world history was the Russian E 0-10-0, which totalled some 14,000 examples, and after

Introduction

these came the German Kriegslokomotive 2-10-0s, the Third Reich's workhorse of World War II; in basic form these totalled more than 6,000 examples. Teutonic precision had ensured earlier standardisations and the Prussian G8 0-8-0 and P8 4-6-0 numbered some 5,000 and 3,000 examples respectively. More recently, the Chinese have achieved comparable figures with their QJ class 2-10-2s, having over 4,000 units in service. These are all dramatic exceptions, however, as the vast majority of designs produced consisted of much smaller numbers, with an average of less than fifty examples per type.

Steam locomotives can be grouped into six basic categories according to the duties they were designed to perform. In order of evolution, the categories are as follows: industrial, freight, express passenger, shunting, suburban and cross country/mixed traffic.

Trains within the industrial category are quite distinct from any main-line operation, being confined to large industrial concerns, such as mines, docks, collieries, iron and steel works, quarries and power stations. Typically, these were small tank engines, but there were many fascinating exceptions to the rule, as the following pages reveal.

The main-line freight locomotive evolved in 1825 when *Locomotion* was used on the Stockton and Darlington Railway. Freight haulers were, by definition, tender engines which ranged from 0-6-0s to 0-8-0s in their formative years to huge 2-10-4s and even larger Mallets at the end of the steam age. Most were characterised by relatively small wheels, designed to provide maximum adhesion when starting with heavy loads.

Express passenger engines were even more highly specialised, and they had large wheels, which were necessary to keep the moving parts running at moderate speeds. The type began with the singles, gravitated to 2-4-0s and 4-4-0s by the end of the nineteenth century, reaching its ultimate in most parts of the world with the Pacific 4-6-2.

Shunting engines evolved with the marshalling yards and large sidings, which were established once railway networks had developed and an interchange of traffic movements became necessary. Like their industrial relations, they were invariably tank engines designed for maximum adhesion and easy manoeuvrability, although many down-graded and out-winded freight engines gravitated into shunting yards in later years.

After the main lines had been built, suburban and cross-country locomotives arrived to service the urban districts around the areas of concentrated manufacturing and commercial activity. Such suburban services were best worked by tank engines, as these were able to run easily in either direction and had small wheels in order to start rapidly after their frequent station stops. Cross-country engines served the secondary interconnecting lines that joined up the main arteries, as well as the branch lines built around the same time. These engines were often similar to those used on suburban work, although in later years many downgraded passenger types found a further lease of active life on these secondary lines.

Mixed traffic was primarily a manifestation of the twentieth century, when freight trains had increased in speed, and rationalisation within motive power fleets demanded engines suitable for a wide range of duties. Such engines ultimately fulfilled most requirements on many of the world's railways, with the exception of the fastest passenger trains and the heaviest of freight hauls.

Examples of all these categories remain active across the world as the revolutionary discovery of steam in nineteenth-century Britain was so far reaching and its consequences so traumatic that its vestiges could never be eradicated in a few years of modernisation. Soon, the steam locomotive will have been a prime mover in the world for more than two centuries, since many years have yet to elapse in some countries before the fires are dropped for the last time. Once everywhere that was anywhere had steam railways, and the veterans linger on in the age of the microchip.

It is to these survivors, the last true workhorses of the Industrial Revolution, that this book is devoted. Sadly, their numbers dwindle daily and always at the cost of diversity and antiquity, for although the steam locomotive's survival into the twenty-first century is assured, this will inevitably be in its more standardised forms. For sure, should it ever come back to the forefront of the world's transport systems, it will not be in the same beloved multiplicity of forms that grace the pages of this book.

MOTIVE POWER DEPOTS

Motive power depots, or engine sheds in common parlance, were the powerhouses of Britain's Industrial Revolution. They were strategically located at important junctions, in large towns and throughout the industrial belts; here, within a space of little more than a few acres, would be concentrated the power for the region's prime transport needs. Motive power depots fulfilled two principal functions: firstly, they were responsible for rostering out locomotives for all the workings within their area, and secondly, they provided routine daily maintenance for the locomotives, as well as periodic servicing and basic repairs.

Each depot had its own allocation of locomotives, and these could range from several hundred at the larger sheds to less than a dozen at the smaller ones. Many large towns and important junctions had separate depots for passenger and freight operations, others in less important areas provided locomotives for a whole range of services. A fine example of motive-power zoning was at Crewe, where the North shed handled the top-link passenger power for the many routes radiating from that junction, whilst Crewe South depot handled the multiplicity of freight and shunting diagrams always associated with any important junction and marshalling yard. In the later years of steam, the tall, mechanical coaling plants were familiar landmarks and ready pointers to the whereabouts of these enchanting places.

Rostering was extremely complex and many locomotives would run for periods of several days, depots on the ongoing section of the various diagrams being responsible for fuelling and routine servicing as necessary.

Few people could fail to be thrilled by the atmosphere and intrigue of the engine sheds. The massive concentration of locomotives in close proximity there was positively awe-inspiring and the omnipresent tension of these gurgling giants unforgettable. These were places of intense and fervent activity, where locomotives coming in for coaling, watering, fireraking, oiling, sanding and turning contrasted with a steady stream of prepared steam locomotives going out to work. All of this happened alongside massive backup facilities that enabled others to receive boiler washouts and more extensive routine maintenance in the Sick Bay, as the repair area of the depot was known.

At the height of the steam age, the railway was the lifeblood of the economy and motive power depots were operative in varying degrees of intensity every day and night of the year. An average depot with an allocation of eighty locomotives would employ hundreds of men on a three-shift system around the clock, ranging from drivers and firemen to fitting staff, shed labourers of many grades, down to the junior cleaners who traditionally were beginning their long apprenticeship to becoming drivers. On the administrative side were the shed foreman and the many grades of chargehands, along with a clerical staff who handled everything from locomotive mileages to drivers' timecards. The whole operation would be under a shed master, who was answerable in turn to the divisional superintendents.

The depots themselves took many fascinating forms; some were round houses with the routes radiating from a common turntable in the centre, others were long houses in which the engines were placed one behind another on any number of tracks, whilst others were half round houses, again with the routes radiating from a common turntable. Whatever the form of depot, a section was always reserved for repairs and maintenance, with most of the really intense activity occurring in the shed yard.

The motive power depot was a creation of the steam age, required partly because of the magnitude of railway operations at that time, but also because of the labour intensiveness of the steam locomotive itself. A considerable number of depots were needed – as recently as 1950 there were over 350 in Britain alone. Today, the prime objective is to have the minimum number of depots, with locomotives constantly out on line, moving from stabling points and only visiting their home depot at infrequent intervals when periodic maintenance has to be carried out. Indeed, the whole emphasis of locomotive design now is to reduce such maintenance by modular construction of parts, the ultimate ideal being to keep locomotives permanently on line for the vast majority of their working lives.

Efficient though this may be, it has deprived the railway of one of its most fascinating aspects, for a concentration of many locomotives on shed comprised of both home engines and visitors, with their exotic aura of faraway places, has always been a source of joy and fascination for young and old alike.

A pair of Indonesian State Railways B51 Class 4-4-0s (facing page) boil up outside their depot at Rangkasbitung, in Northern Java. These oil-fired veterans are among the world's last outside cylinder 4-4-0s and clearly show their Prussian ancestry. The flags on the smoke box top of No. B5138 are part of the celebrations for Independence Day.

Above: two British thoroughbreds on shed at Olavarria, on the former Buenos Aires and Great Southern Railway network in Argentina. The one on the left is a IIA Class 2-8-0, alongside one of the splendid 15B Class 4-8-0s. The tragic decline of this once-magnificent railway is clearly in evidence, for the pride of the BAGS has been decimated by the petty profiteering of road hauliers with vested interests and by fifth column practices. The Scottish ancestry of this IIB Class 2-8-0 (right) is in full evidence, albeit that this example was one of the last batch delivered and came from the Vulcan Foundry at Newton-le-Willows, Lancashire, in 1931.

Left: a lively scene at the Sabero colliery in Northern Spain depicting a vintage Sharpe Stewart 0-6-0T *El Esla* of 1878 on the left, standing alongside an 0-6-0T built by Couillet of Belgium. This metre-gauge system is one of steam's last strongholds in Spain. Although steam building finished in India in 1972, major overhauls continue to this day. One of the principal works is in Jamalpur, where (bottom left) an HGS Class 2-8-0, descended from the BESA period, is seen alongside a WP Class Pacific. The two engines are preparing for running trials from Jamalpur shed, having received major overhauls. Two BESA-styled classics (below) at Lucknow receive the detailed embellishments so characteristic of Indian locomotives. The inside cylinder 0-6-0 on the left was built by Armstrong Whitworth of Newcastle-upon-Tyne in 1923, whilst the HPS Class 4-6-0 on the right came from the Vulcan Foundry in 1950. The once vast Howrah steam sheds in Calcutta had, until the late '70s, classic British designs both from the BESA and X series. Overleaf: an inside cylinder 0-6-0 *Maid of all Work* reposes alongside one of the magnificent XC Class Pacifics, introduced in 1928.

Above: sunset at Tubarão sheds on Brazil's metre-gauge Teresa Cristina Railway reveals a 2-6-6-0 Mallet and two of the system's smaller Mikados – all from the Baldwin stable. Right: sunrise at Burdwan Depot in Bengal, the last home of Indian Railways' XC Class Pacifics. Two are seen here with an American-inspired WG Class 2-8-2 (right), the type which ultimately displaced them from shunting and pick-up freight duties. Overleaf: the Sunday stoker, shovel in hand, flits between an array of gurgling giants on Brazil's Teresa Cristina Railway as he tends the fires and tops the boilers with water in readiness for the new week's workings.

One of China's finest steam centres is Harbin (above), in the north east of the country. Until the recent infiltration of diesels, the depot had an allocation of a hundred steam locomotives, of which most were QJs for working long distance freight trains, particularly to the south along the main line through Manchuria. Top right: locomotive utilisation is highly impressive; servicing activities are carried out with great rapidity and the engines returned to the main line with minimum delay. Right: the JS Class Mikado 2-8-2, one of the QJ's smaller sisters, reposes alongside an even smaller SY Class industrial Mikado.

Left: a scene in the depot yard at Howrah in Calcutta reveals three celebrated designs for India's 5ft 6in gauge lines. On the right is BESA period SGC2 Class Inside Cylinder 0-6-0, No. 34175, built by the Vulcan Foundry in 1913 for the East Indian Railway. In the centre stands XC Class Pacific No. 22228, a Vulcan Foundry engine of 1928, while on the left rests WP Pacific No. 7726, a Chittaranjan engine of 1966. Here are the three principal phases of twentieth-century broad-gauge locomotive development – the BESA period, the X series period and the final American Standards period – plus an interesting contrast between the British Thoroughbred Pacific of the 1920s and the American version of twenty years later. Below: a line-up of WP Class Pacifics in the shed yard at Lucknow. All are diagrammed to take express passenger trains and are part of this depot's large allocation of American Pacifics. Facing page: a brace of Turkish State Railways' Skyliner 2-10-0s boil up outside their depot at Irmak prior to heading freight trains northward to Zonguldak, on the Black Sea coast. Eighty-eight of these powerful locomotives were delivered to Turkey from the Vulcan Ironworks at Wilkes Barre in Pennsylvania between 1947 and 1949.

One of Britain's last great industrial systems was based around Dalmellington in Ayrshire, where a stud of Andrew Barclay saddle tanks survived on various duties until the mid '70s. An ironworks was built in Dalmellington in 1845 and was served by collieries in the immediate area, which survived long after the foundries were closed down. The system connected with British Railways at Waterside, the site of the former ironworks – the most outlying colliery being at Pennyvenie, where West Ayr Area No. 21 (above), a standard 16in Andrew Barclay 0-4-0ST, can be seen sedately drawing a rake of freshly lifted coals. Notice that the first wagon is non-standard and is serving as an improvised tender for additional fuel capacity.

ENGINES OF BRITISH INDUSTRY

The industrial locomotive is quite distinct from its main-line counterpart and saw use in such places as collieries, quarries, foundries, docks, coking plants, power stations and large factories. These engines were seldom seen by the public at large, often being confined to industrial establishments off the beaten track or else lost within the maze of foundries and factories that were the central features of the major manufacturing belts of Britain. The world's first steam locomotive was an industrial. Built at an ironworks in South Wales in 1804, it was designed to convey iron to a canal basin for shipment by barge to the docks. A few years later, industrial engines began to appear on the coalfields of Yorkshire and Northumberland.

The origin of the industrial locomotive lay in the small engines built for the contractors who undertook the massive programme of construction throughout the 'railway mania' of the 1840s. These engines were needed to supplement the muscle power of the navvies and horses when building cuttings, embankments, tunnels, viaducts and stations. They had to be compact and economical, able to work over temporary track, negotiate tight curves and yet have sufficient adhesion to draw heavy trainloads of earth and materials. Additionally, the engines had to be easy to transport from one site to another. Small tank engines met all these requirements.

Once the main lines were laid, the Industrial Revolution progressed with increased velocity; enormous quantities of iron and coal were required and these very industries needed the same type of locomotives as the contractors did. Thus, by 1850, the industrial steam locomotive, as it appears in these pages, had evolved.

The basic form was a side or a saddle tank, which had either four or six coupled wheels (0-4-0 and 0-6-0) with two cylinders, usually placed inside the frame. Outside cylinder versions did occur, particularly on the four-wheelers, where the short boiler provided insufficient room for a crank axle. These engines changed little throughout their evolution, growing within moderate limits both in terms of power output and size, and seldom exceeding fifty tonnes in weight.

Industrial engines are associated with the towns in which their builders were located. In Scotland, the coal and ironstone reserves of Ayrshire gave work to builders in Kilmarnock, pre-eminent amongst whom was Andrew Barclay, who produced highly distinctive locomotives for almost a century.

In Newcastle-upon-Tyne Robert Stephenson and Hawthorn Leslie both produced highly distinctive designs, but the true home of the industrial locomotive was Leeds, where in the tiny parish of Hunslet there were four celebrated builders: Manning Wardle, Hudswell Clarke, Kitsons and Hunslet. Further south, in Stafford, William Bagnall readily tailored his designs to customer requirements and as a result this company's list contains some of the most delightful variations ever played on the conventional theme. Meanwhile, in the deep south, a distinctive family of engines arose from the designs of Peckett and Avonside in Bristol.

Sadly, the combination of closures, rationalisations in plant layouts and the increasing use of trucks and overhead cranes within all aspects of heavy industry has lead to a drastic decline in the number of locations using industrials, as has the the main-line railway's use of merry-go-round trains to service industries such as power stations and collieries direct. So although steam survived in industry for some years after it had disappeared from mainline service, diesels rapidly encroached on the surviving locations and today, after almost two centuries of operation, the industrial locomotive is extinct in Britain. These engines preceded their main-line counterparts by some twenty years and survived them by approximately the same timespan.

Leicester Power Station's magnificent Robert Stephenson and Hawthorn 0-4-0 saddle tank (facing page) gently backs a rake of loaded wagons from the British Rail Exchange into the power station hoppers. She was built as recently as 1950 to a Hawthorn Leslie design dating from the early years of the century. She has twelve-inch-diameter cylinders, and slide valves operated by Stephenson's link motion. Castle Donington Power Station, also in Leicestershire, is home to a pair of blue-liveried RSH 0-4-0STs, also descended from an earlier Hawthorn Leslie design. The family likeness between the Hawthorn 0-4-0 saddle tank and the RSH 0-4-0ST (above) is unmistakable, although the latter has sixteen-inch-diameter cylinders. This powerful 0-6-0T (right), seen towards the end of her working life in the Glenboig colliery in Glasgow, comes from the Leeds school of industrial locomotive development, having originally come from Hudswell Clarke in 1909.

The one-and-three-quarter-century-long tradition of steam and coal – the lifeblood of the industrial revolution – ended in Britain during the early 1980s at the Cadley Hill colliery on the Derbyshire coalfield. Among Cadley Hill's fleet was *Empress* (above), a standard 16in Bagnall design which first appeared in 1944, although descended from an earlier similar design. Two other members (left) of Cadley Hill's fleet can still be seen, a Hunslet Austerity on the left, *Cadley Hill No 1*, alongside *Progress*, a Robert Stephenson and Hawthorn 0-6-0 saddle tank, built in Newcastle in 1946. As with the 0-4-0s on previous pages, she is also descended from an earlier Hawthorn Leslie design and is unusual in having inside cylinders. *Cadley Hill No 1* (facing page) was one of the last three Hunslet Austerities to be built and didn't emerge from Hunslet's Leeds works until 1962. The Hunslet Austerity was specially designed for operations during World War II, after which many passed to the metals of the newly formed National Coal Board, to become a standard design and ultimately the last working steam locomotives in Britain.

Beneath a magnificent layer of grime, a vintage Andrew Barclay 0-6-0 saddle tank of 1900 (above) pauses at the British Railways exchange for a blow up, having drawn a rake of loaded wagons from the Polkemment colliery in West Lothian. The crane tank was a form of industrial which combined an ability to shunt works yards with an ability to load wagons and move heavy items around the various fabrication shops. Among Britain's last working examples is the 0-4-0 CT (right) which survived, with a few others, at Doxford's shipyard in Pallion, Sunderland, until 1971.

ENGINES OF WORLD INDUSTRY

In world terms, the industrial locomotive differed considerably from those confined to Britain. Generally they were more powerful, as wagon sizes were often heavier than those in Britain and the industries themselves invariably larger. Britain's small size, combined with her diversity of industries, which developed piecemeal under private enterprise during the formative years of the Industrial Revolution, had much to do with this. Small industrial units serving a densely populated area of heavy manufacturing were sustainable, but in less developed countries, industries tended to be larger, more spread out and located at longer distances from the mainline railway. This, combined with poor and often heavily graded track, necessitated a very different kind of locomotive from the homely British saddletank that worked at the local gasworks.

Many world industrials were, of course, similar to their British counterparts in terms of power output, and Britain did export such locomotives to many lands. On a world canvas, these readily mixed with a massive quantity of German engines from such pre-eminent builders as Orenstein and Koppel, with their huge family of characteristically shaped designs, as well as with those locomotives from American plants as large as Baldwins, to the smaller foundries that specialised in industrials, like Lima of Ohio. Although industrial locomotives were used across the world in similar establishments to the ones in Britain, there are two additional major locations – sugar plantations and logging lines – which even today rely on steam locomotives to convey their raw materials from the cutting areas to the factories. These systems are invariably built to narrow gauges ranging from 2ft 6in to 3ft 6in.

Some of the world's largest industrials occur in South Africa, where the main-line gauge is only 3ft 6in, but here it is free of the loading gauge restrictions that apply in more developed areas of the world. This enables locomotives and rolling stock to be built higher and wider, as often the coalfield hauls are heavier than were the average main-line hauls in Europe at the end of steam – and this over track beds that are often much more steeply graded. Many of these locomotives are former mainliners and, as such, reveal another fascinating category of industrials: the engines that have seen service, either on the privately owned or state main-line systems, and are pensioned off into industry for a further lease of active life. This cross-fertilisation of different types of locomotives was aided by the steady increase in tonnages – thus an engine built in the late-nineteenth century to handle the heaviest main-line freight hauls of the day was inadequate fifty years later. These engines are either demoted to lighter work, such as tripping and shunting, or else offered for sale to industrial users as an alternative to being broken up.

Through this method, many historic types which would otherwise have become extinct long since have lingered in industrial establishments, sometimes for incredibly long periods of time. As the stresses and demands upon an industrial can be relatively modest, given good maintenance many seem to go on forever. Large mainline engines seldom penetrated the ranks of British industry, but they certainly made inroads elsewhere; in Africa, Latin America, on the Indian subcontinent and in China many large locomotives, some of them extremely powerful, have found a new lease of life. These contrast magnificently with the traditional, smaller designs, providing a tapestry of interesting locomotives across a rich diversity of locations.

The stone railway at Gunung Kataren, Sumatra, was one of the world's most remarkable industrial lines. Its purpose was to convey stones from the river bed up to the crushing plant in order to provide track ballast for the island's mainline railways. The smooth stones are clearly visible as engine No. 106 (above), an 0-6-0T built in 1926 by Ducroo and Brauns of Weesp, Holland, prepares to back a loaded train to the crushers.

The yellow-flowering trees of Java make a fine backdrop for *Bromo* (above), an Orenstein and Kopell 0-8-0 tender tank of 1913, as it works for the Purwodadi sugar factory in the eastern part of the island, its tender piled high with cubes of bagasse . Another German-built industrial, a diminutive 600mm gauge 0-4-0 well tank (top right), also from Orenstein and Kopell, heads a loaded train from a stone quarry in central Uruguay. The barrel precariously perched atop the boiler indicates that she is an oil burner. Right: the world's last Kitson Meyer 0-6-6-0T at Taltal, in Chile's Atacama Desert. Notice the rear chimney protruding from the bunker and exhausting steam from the rear cylinders.

One of South Africa's most fascinating and antiquated industrials was Albion colliery's No. 3 (above), a hybridised 4-8-0 tender engine rebuilt from a 13 Class 4-10-2T supplied by Neilson of Glasgow in 1902. Top right: a very different No. 3 at the East Daggafontein goldmine. Originally a mainliner, she was a member of the Natal Government Railway A Class, which consisted of a hundred engines built by the Dubs works in Queens Park, Glasgow, between 1888 and 1900. Right: another former Natal Government Railway Class A, active on the Grootvlei Proprietary Mines goldfield at Springs, in the Transvaal.

Vast reserves of iron ore underlie India's Bihar Province, and these feed the great iron and steel works on the eastern coalfield of Bengal. At Manoharpur, two Andrew Barclay 0-6-2Ts (below) head along the branch from the mines to the South Eastern Railway's main line. Right: the Indian Iron and Steel Corporation's Burnpur works in Bengal, where No. 9, a 2-6-0T built by Nasmyth Wilson of Patricroft, Manchester, waits for the cauldron to be filled. Bottom right: No. 17, a heavy-duty 0-6-0 tank built by Robert Stephenson and Hawthorn in 1948, also in the Burnpur works.

These pages: slag tipping at Karabuk steelworks, northern Turkey. A stream of molten waste (top left) pours down a bank as one of Karabuk's stud of British-built 0-6-0 saddle tanks eases the wagons into place. She was built in 1948 by Robert Stephenson and Hawthorn, but is descended from an earlier Hawthorn Leslie design delivered for the steelworks' opening in 1937. Left: one of the huge Bagnall 0-8-0s performs a spectacular night tip. Above: a Robert Stephenson and Hawthorn 0-6-0ST of 1948. Although the huge moulded forms of solidified slag have cooled on the outside, in many cases their centres are still liquid. Overleaf: the striking contrasts of slag-tipping at twilight, with the typical shape of a Hawthorn Leslie engine, virtually identical to that builder's designs for British industrial establishments, silhouetted against the early evening sky.

These pages: JF Class Mikado No. 841 heads an engineers' train during slewing operations at Zalainoer near Manzhouli. Mining here centres upon a great open-cast pit, where lines zig-zag down to a depth of 250 feet, along terraces thirty feet in depth. The tracks are slewed in accordance with the mining operation as the pit gradually spreads outwards across the landscape.

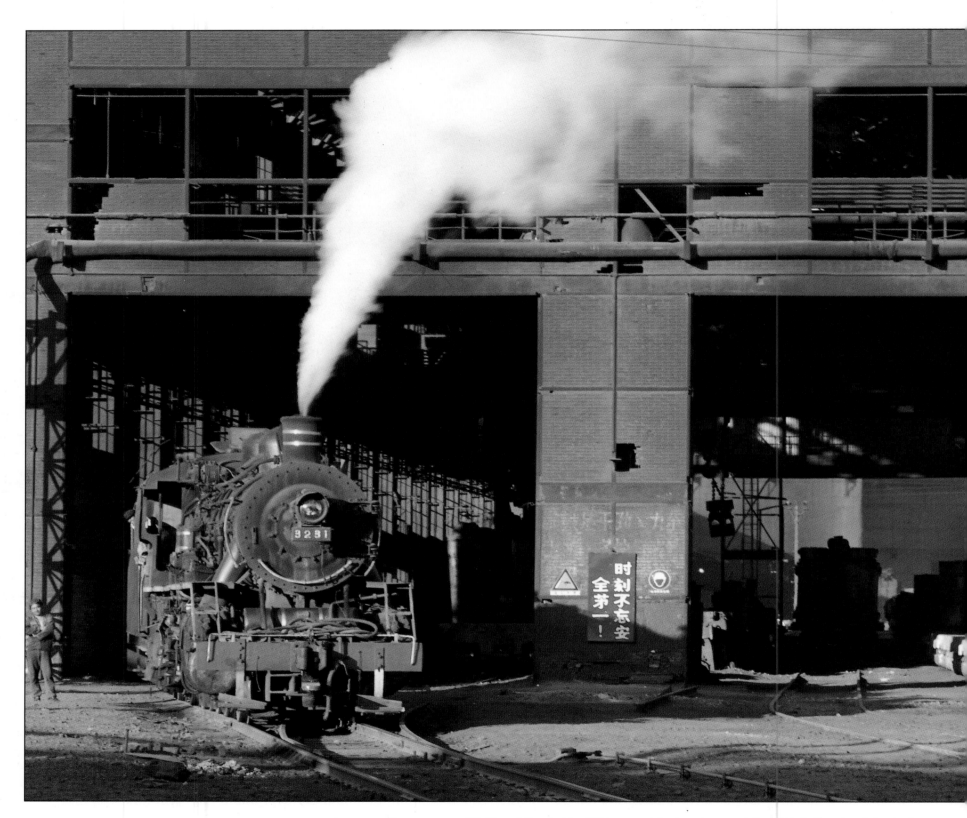

These pages: JF6 Class Mikado No. 3231, one of Anshan Iron and Steel Works' most celebrated survivors. The type is descended from a standard Alco design and made its appearance on the South Manchurian and Manchuria National Railways during the 1930s. Although they were built in large numbers, very few are found in mainline service, as their modest proportions have now been surpassed by greatly increased train weights. It is thought that many JF6s were rebuilt to form the industrial PL2 Class Prairie 2-6-2 by fitting a shorter boiler and removing the last coupled axle. China's present-day SY Class, which continues to be built at Tangshan, is based directly on the JF6 and is virtually identical in dimensions and power output.

Above: two of the Hawaiian-Philippine Company's 3ft gauge Red Dragons stand alongside the control office prior to beginning the night shift. By the middle of the evening they will have left for the plantation, to return with loaded trains in the early hours. During the intensely busy milling season, the railroad runs for twenty-four hours, six days a week – Sunday being set aside for servicing and cleaning. Depicted here are Dragons Nos. 3 and 5, both of which were built by Baldwin in 1920. Dragon No. 3, on the left, is a bagasse burner, as her huge, balloon stack chimney indicates, while Dragon No. 5 has a slender stovepipe chimney, indicating that she is an oil burner. During the early part of the season, some locomotives burn oil until sufficient bagasse has been accrued.

AMERICAN INDUSTRIAL ENGINES – ON THE PLANTATIONS

Many of the survivors in plantation service bear a generic resemblance to the early phases of development. Today, only three countries hold a representative selection: Cuba, the Philippines and Brazil. Cuba is by far the most important, and can be regarded as the last major haven of American steam traction on earth. Before the Revolution in 1959, the island was to all intents under American rule and the rapid development of the sugar industry during the nineteenth century gave rise to a prolific export business of locomotives from the USA, both for mainline and plantation service. The Revolution brought Fidel Castro to power and ousted the American puppet dictator, Batista. Fidel's communist administration brought a swift and hostile reaction from America and all connections with Cuba were severed – a situation which remains the same today, thirty years later. This has left a huge reserve of American locomotives frozen in time; had the Revolution not taken place, diesels would have made a rapid incursion, but the delicate nature of Cuba's economy – not least because of the American embargo – has ensured steam's survival.

Cuba is the world's largest sugar exporter, with over 150 mills on the island, well over a third of which are known to use steam railroads. In most cases these are confined to the mills and plantations, but larger engines do work considerable distances over Cuba Railway's fully dieselized main lines as part of their journey from outlying plantations to the mills. This is a rare practice, for seldom does one find industrials in service over mainline networks. Many of the cane hauls are extremely heavy and the sight of early-twentieth-century 2-8-0s toiling over steep gradients with massive trains is one of the last great manifestations of American steam. Add to this the sonorous call of chime whistles and the ringing of bells against the backdrop of wooden signal boxes on stilts guarding semaphores and flat crossings, and one has a tapestry which could have been almost anywhere in the US during the early years of the present century.

Another unusual feature of sugar railway operation in Cuba is the proliferation of standard gauge lines in accordance with the mainline system, although smaller gauges do exist, including 3ft and 2ft 6in, along with examples of the more unusual 2ft 3¾in, and 2ft 7¾in. The motive power fleet is extremely diverse. Some of the standard gauge examples were actually exported secondhand from America's railroads, others are ex Cuba Railways main lines, while the remainder are typical exports from the great builders, with such legendary names as Baldwin, ALCO, Porter, Rodgers and Davenport all being represented.

The island's largest type is the 1900 Class 2-8-0 and this is the most common wheel arrangement, but also represented in great diversity are 2-6-0s, 2-6-2s, 4-6-0s and 4-6-2s, along with 0-6-0 and 0-4-0 Saddle Tanks. Almost every mill has a random assortment of locomotives, all quite different, no attempt at standardisation ever having been made – nor could it have been in view of the wide diversity of gauges and sources from which the engines have been obtained. Among the island's more distinctive survivors are a remarkable Porter 0-4-4 suburban tank, believed to have come from a New York elevated railway, along with a fine range of vintage Baldwin Saddle Tanks. The oldest engine on the island is an 0-4-2 proudly bearing a plate which claims she hailed from Baldwin's works, Philadelphia, in 1878.

Unique in world service are the American Fireless engines which survive at several mills. The Fireless was one of the most significant variations ever played on the conventional theme and is distinctive in taking its steam direct from the boilers of the factory. One charge at high pressure enables the engines to work effectively on yard movements, usually pushing cane into the crushers, and placing the empty wagons back onto the sidings. Such engines are ideal for those industries with a ready supply of steam as part of their manufacturing process. The Fireless is an American innovation – the first examples are believed to have operated in 1873 on a three-and-a-half-mile line running from East New York to Canarsie in Brooklyn, N.Y.

The Philippines represent another important haven of thoroughbred American design. Here, as in Cuba, the sugar industry was developed by the US. Many railroads were built to the small gauge of either 3ft or 3ft 6in, and the survivors are concentrated on Negros Island, where companies like the Hawaii Philippines have now become world famous for their 'Red Dragons'. The black engines of La Carlotta have also become justifiably renowned, as were the decrepit, battered, multi-hued relics of Ma ao Sugar Central until their recent demise. In Cuba, the preferred form of fuel is oil, whereas the Philippine systems invariably use bagasse. This is sugar cane waste – the dry fibres of the crushed cane which in baled form make an excellent locomotive fuel. Although low in calorific value, and requiring two firemen, bagasse does sustain small locomotives and avoids the costly importation of oil, which would use up valuable foreign exchange.

The sugar railways of Brazil, in common with those of the Philippines, have declined in recent years. The motive power fleet is varied, and the American veterans mix with British and German examples, but in the Campos and Pernambuco areas of the country moderately sized locomotives can be found on various gauges sporting many of the great US foundries on their maker's plates. Interestingly, Brazil's sugar railroads have a tradition of using wood-fired locomotives, emphasising the ability of steam traction to burn a variety of available fuels. This, combined with the tough, rugged designs, has ensured the survival of these stalwarts far beyond the timespan that their designers would have envisaged.

The passing years inevitably bring many casualties, not least in Cuba, where Russian diesels are now making their presence felt, but it seems likely that a few sugar plantations will still be reverberating to the bark of America's Iron Horse into the twenty-first century.

Porter, Baldwin, Alco and Vulcan, these were the names that spread the fame of America's locomotive builders throughout the world. Now rusted and tarnished, these works plates are to be found on working engines in the most remote locations. Overleaf: oil-burning Dragon No. 7, made by Baldwin in 1928, darkens the plantations as she waits to collect a loaded train.

Above: No. 1907, a Baldwin 2-8-0 of July 1924, heads towards the connection with Cuba Railways' main line. This engine is part of the roster at Carlos Manuel de Céspedes Sugar Mill, in Cuba's Camaguey Province. Lighter operations at Carlos Manuel de Céspedes are performed by a delightful Porter Mogul of 1919 (right). Based in Pittsburgh, Pennsylvania, Porter was America's leading industrial locomotive builder, their engines readily identifiable from their shield-shaped works plates.

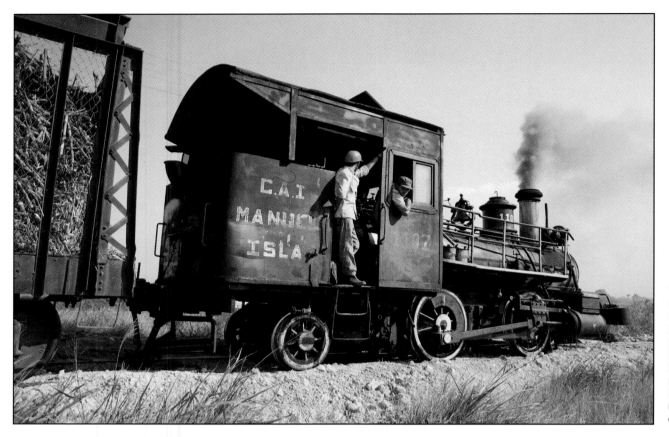

Left: a delightful well tank, one of Cuba's oldest locomotives. She works at the Manuel Isla Perez Sugar Mill, to which she was delivered new from Baldwin in 1882. Running with the precision of a well-oiled sewing machine, she seems fit to work another century. Below: an 0-4-0 saddle tank, another lovely Baldwin, completed at the Philadelphia works in July 1919 to an older design – notice the crosshead-driven feed pump for injecting water into the boiler. Facing page: a metre-gauge Baldwin 2-8-0 leaves the mill with a train of empties bound for Conselheiro Josino, a journey that will involve running over the RFFSA main line. Delivered in 1894 for Brazil's Leopoldina Railways, she passed from mainline to sugar plantation service to work on the Outeiro Usina in Brazil's Campos Province. Overleaf: bagasse-burning Dragon No. 6 trundles a rake of empties along the Magasa Line. The Hawaiian-Philippine Company's network is made up of several main lines, totalling around a hundred route miles.

Above: one of Eduardo G. Lavendero sugar mill's stud of five standard-gauge Baldwin 2-8-0s prepares to leave for the cane fields. She was built as Baldwin No. 52913 in February, 1920. These are the engines that bring the heavy rakes of cane in from the plantations for transference to the system's 0-4-0 saddle tank for conveyance to the crushers. In common with most of Cuba's steam fleet, No. 1805 is an oil burner, since the island has no indigenous coal reserves and bagasse produces insufficient heat to power heavy trains. Right: Brazil's Usina Outeiro's Baldwin 2-8-0 No. 7 heads along the RFFSA main line between Conselheiro Josino and Marundu with a load of sugar cane.

Above left: a pair of Baldwin-built Fireless engines await their next turn of duty at Bolivia Mill in Cuba. In front is No. 1169, an 0-4-0F of 1917 and behind, smaller sister No. 1170 of 1916. Left: in this detailed study of No. 1169, the feed valve, which takes steam from the sugar mill's boilers, can be seen in front of the rear wheels – the supply to the cylinders is made through the centre pipe at the front, while the exhaust steam issues from the vertical pipes alongside. Above: a Baldwin 0-4-0 Fireless No. 1131 of 1916 from Espartico Mill in Cienfuegos Province, Cuba, makes a marvellous contrast with the examples at Bolivia. The Fireless was arguably the most efficient and economical shunting unit ever devised and was ideal for any industry with a ready supply of high-pressure steam. The engines are subject to a relatively low amount of stress and they require no fuel and hardly any maintenance – in effect, a Fireless will run for an entire season for just a pot of oil and the driver's wages. The world's last American-built Fireless locomotives are now to be found in Cuba.

Above: a Baldwin-built 4-6-0T from World War 1, she is the Upper Indian Sugar Mills 60cm (23½ in) gauge network's No. 2, seen here taking refreshment prior to returning to the mill with a loaded train. Until fairly recently the bullock was second only to Indian Railways in the movement of tonnage on the sub-continent. Above right: Ma Ao Sugar Central No. 5, a spritely Mogul built by Alco in 1924, approaches the mill with a loaded train. She is paired with a tender from a condemned locomotive – notice the corrugated iron sheeting for keeping the bagasse dry during the typhoons which regularly lash Negros Island during the milling season. The BM on her cab-side indicates that she formerly belonged to the Bacolod and Murcia Milling Company, long since closed. Right: a Baldwin 4-6-0T belonging to the Upper Indian Sugar Mills pictured in a typical rural environment. Overleaf: Ma Ao Sugar Central's charming 0-6-2, un-numbered and unidentified, gently easing empty cane cars into one of the many loading sidings.

These pages: rural scenes depicting 60cm (23½in) gauge Baldwin-built 4-6-0Ts, which are ending their days amid the tranquillity of the Upper Indian Sugar Mills plantations.

Above: old Shay No. 12, a three-truck, three-cylinder veteran from Lima of Ohio dating from 1907, gently backs a heavy rake of mahogany trunks into position at the Maaslud Exchange sidings of the Insular Lumber Company on the Philippine island of Negros. No. 12, the largest of Insular Lumber's Shays, was used in the mountains for conveying logs from the cutting area to the exchange sidings ready for the journey down to the saw mill. Five other Shays on Insular Lumber's roster tripped around the saw mills during their final years.

AMERICAN INDUSTRIAL LOCOMOTIVES –
ON THE LOGGING LINES

Logging was another major industry in which the American steam locomotive played an important part, and the traditions of the Pacific Northwest spread to other lands. It is a form of railroading which has now disappeared, but its final flowering in the Philippines possessed all the rustic drama and fullbloodedness one associates with so arduous an industry. Many of the great logging systems closed as the woods were economically depleted, a few succumbed to dieselization, but the majority are now centred around trucking routes. Railway logging survives in Russia and China, where many systems remain, but with motive power descended from Russian practice.

The highly specialized nature of the early railways demanded a specific form of motive power; conventional locomotives were inadequate for the curved, tortuous tracks invariably engulfed in a sea of mud. In America, these problems were solved by the Shay, one of the most fascinating variations ever played on the conventional locomotive. It was the brainchild of Ephrame Shay, a backwoods logging engineer, and was adopted by the Lima Locomotive Works of Ohio, who took out a patent on the design and produced the vast majority of the three thousand subsequently built.

The Shay is flexibly mounted on four-wheel bogies known as trucks. The cylinders are set in a vertical position on the engine's right-hand side and drive a horizontal crankshaft running the length of the locomotive, the drive being applied by pinions slotting into beveled gears on the truck wheels. This single crankshaft is made flexible by the incorporation of universal joints. Gearing the engine in this way, combined with small wheels, gives an even turning movement and avoids slipping when working heavy trains over muddy tracks. Shays were inevitably slow, but a steady, reliable speed of ten miles an hour fulfilled their function well enough. Most consisted of two or perhaps three trucks, although four-truck examples did exist in which the additional truck carried an extra fuel tender. Shays are referred to by their combination of cylinders and trucks, as in the three-cylinder/two-truck variety. The last of the Shays vanished from the metals of the legendary Insular Lumber Company on the Philippine island of Negros. This railroad had an amazing fleet of Shays working with a huge 0-6-6-0 Baldwin Mallet of 1925. The Mallet worked the main line from the logging sidings down to the sawmill, while the Shays brought the logs from the cutting areas to the exchange sidings and also tripped around the mill. Watching them was unforgettable; the roaring cylinders were matched by the grinding cacophony of gears as the wheels bounced over uneven trackbeds, the gnashing and crashing doubtless accentuated by wear in the axle boxes. The noise, combined with their incredible shape, provided a unique experience, especially at night, when the huge spark-arresting chimneys – improvised from cut down oil drums – emitted flurries of brightly coloured mahogany embers which sprayed the tropical vegetation with all the force of an erupting Roman candle.

At the exchange sidings, far up in the hills, old Shay No. 12 of 1907, a three-cylinder, three-truck variety from Lima, rasped her way through the sea of mud with a heavy rake of mahogany. She stood waiting until the break of dawn, when the big Mallet arrived from the sawmill with the empties, and for a few moments the two antiquities stood side by side in the half-light, curling wisps of crimson embers against the dawning sky. Their incredible silhouettes, blazing headlights and fearsome whistles conjured up everything that was wild and magnificent in American railroading. As the sun came up, the big Mallet set off with her loaded train, emitting the most grotesque sounds from her four cylinders, all of which had their valves out of alignment. Slipping, coughing and wheezing, the incredible apparition rounded the bend and headed toward the wooden trestle viaduct, built in traditional Wild West manner under American colonial rule. The silvery tones of her chime whistle rang through the mountain groves like a cold shiver as she crossed the viaduct, an active volcano towering beyond her. Once the Mallet had gone, Shay No. 12 picked up a rake of empties and, in a flurry of steam and sparks, propelled them back to the cutting area. So ended the great American logging tradition on that remote Philippine island with two forms of locomotive that will always be associated with the very best of American railroading traditions.

These scenes of the world's last Shays depict the engine's right-hand side, on which the cylinders are conventionally placed. The ratio of gear reduction varies from two to one to three to one, and a three-cylinder engine with cranks set at 120 degrees will have twelve to eighteen impulses per revolution of the wheel. This gives a more even turning movement than an ordinary, two-cylinder engine driving a crankshaft direct, when there are only four impulses per revolution of the wheel. The crankshafts are connected to the pinion shafts by universal joints, as clearly seen in the picture below. Left: No. 15, a two-cylinder two-truck variety from the fine stud of Lima Shays belonging to the Ali Shan Logging Railway in Taiwan, some of which survived until the late 1970s. Below: Insular Lumber Company's Shay No. 1 gently raises steam in the yard of the locomotive depot at Fabrica prior to commencing a day's tripping around the mill. Facing page: Lopez Sugar Central's three-cylinder, three-truck Shay No. 10 emerges from the banana groves with a loaded train. This engine, the last Shay in regular use on the Philippine island of Negros, was purchased by Lopez Sugar when the Insular Lumber Company's operation in Fabrica closed down. Overleaf: Insular Lumber Company's four-cylinder compound 0-6-6-0 Mallet No. 7 slowly draws a loaded train over the Maaslud Viaduct.

Above: one of the Indonesian State Railway B53 Class 4-4-0s. These were superheated versions of the earlier B51 Class and were built for the 3ft 6in gauge Staats Spoorwegen. The class numbered eleven examples, delivered from Hartmann of Germany in 1912 and Werkspoor of Holland in 1914. Once the express locomotives of the Dutch East Indies, the last B53s ended their days working indiscriminately with the older B50 Class Sharp Stewart 2-4-0s on the lightly laid branch from Madiun to Ponorogo and Slahung.

COALING, WATERING AND MAINTAINING

Many indictments have been made against steam traction during the second half of the twentieth century, but perhaps the most damning is the labour-intensive maintenance it demands. Unlike the internal combustion engine, it does not start at the touch of a button, but only after the fire has been lit, and it is many hours before steam is finally raised. Alongside this are the attendant activities of fireraking, coaling, watering and regular oiling for every trip. Equally, the steam locomotive does not switch off when its duty roster is completed; a decision has to be made whether to drop the fire or keep the engine in light steam until it is needed again. Light steam maintenance demands that the engine be visited regularly in order to keep the fire banked up and the boiler topped with water, but so time-consuming is the process of raising steam that this constant use of energy and manpower is the preferred alternative to dropping the fire if a locomotive is needed within the following twelve hours or so.

The situation was made even more complex at the end of every run, as then a locomotive would have to be replenished with coal – sometimes as much as ten tonnes. It had to be watered, have its fire raked and ashpan cleaned, and the deposits of char shovelled from the smoke box. Also, in the majority of cases, the locomotive would have to be turned, and all these operations necessitated going to a depot. The availability of water throughout the railway network was not usually a problem in developed countries, but it could be in many parts of the developing world, and, of course, the movement of vast tonnages of coal from the areas of production to every motive power depot across the country was in itself a massive and costly operation. Some of these difficulties were minimised by the introduction of water troughs between the tracks, from which the engines scooped up water at speed, whilst mechanical coaling plants, rocking grates and self-cleaning smokeboxes were all attributes of latter-day steam practice, as was the introduction of oil-firing. Nevertheless, such labour intensiveness was inherent, for once an engine had left a depot, having been sent on its way by a multifarious workforce, it demanded the constant attention of a driver and fireman.

Air pollution – an emotive issue in the developed world following World War II – was another factor in the decline of steam traction there. The steam locomotive was seen as part of the blackened (and thus unacceptable) legacy from the days of the 'Dark Satanic Mills'. After the war, serious competition from road transportation reared its ugly head, forcing railway networks to modernise and present a new image of competitiveness. This could hardly be achieved as long as trains were hauled by soot-laden, clanking monsters that belched smoke and fumes into the atmosphere. In Western countries, the dirty work associated with running a steam railway also became unfashionable; it was considered unreasonable for a man to be obliged to stand for hours shovelling tonnes of coal in clammy heat on a bucking locomotive or, equally, to suffer the dust and fumes involved in fireraking. Steam locomotive depots, characterised by their pall of smoke mushrooming skywards, became blots on the landscape in a world suddenly conscious of pollution. Additionally, the postwar years were a time of cheap oil, but ever more expensive coal; in many countries a ready availability of high quality steam coal was becoming increasingly difficult to guarantee.

If all these factors are considered against the availability of diesel and electric traction, the utilisation figures for steam compare unfavourably; after all, one diesel can do the work of almost three steam locomotives.

However, steam traction has many pluses: it is cheap to build, simple to maintain and incredibly reliable. It will continue to work well under conditions of adversity that no other form of traction would tolerate – and however bad its ailments, a steam locomotive will almost invariably drag the train home. This contrasts markedly with diesel or electrical traction, where a small technical failure can paralyse a locomotive, or even a whole system. These factors are important in developing countries, where the maintenance of modern forms of traction frequently causes serious problems, but perhaps the fundamental factor in steam traction's favour is the spirit which the steam locomotive generates in man. It is an animated, living machine comprising the fundamental elements of fire and water. Each locomotive has an individual personality to which man can readily respond, and as such it presents a challenge to him, and almost always brings out the best in him. One example of this is the way that a late-running train can be returned to schedule by the driver and firemen coaxing the locomotive to a stupendous performance, much as a skilled jockey coaxes a racehorse. All this introduces an esprit de corps which must be at the heart of any great industry; this and the steam locomotive's capacity to inspire workforce, travelling public and layman alike are facts which are readily forgotten by economists and accountants. The spirit, the dedication and the loyalties once inspired by steam are absent on the modern railways of today and the industry is very much the poorer as a consequence.

Left: a Yugoslav State Railway B51 Class 2-6-2T takes water at Vrginmost as it travels along the lightly laid branch from Sisak to Karlovac. Above: a former Rhodesian Railways 2-6-2+2-6-2 Garratt takes water at Balla Balla, on the West Nicholson to Bulawayo line. As the giant takes refreshment, the blow-down valve is simultaneously opened to eject sludge from the boiler. Eighteen of these 132-tonne giants were exported from Beyer Peacock's works in Gorton, Manchester, between 1953 and 1954. Overleaf: No. 6024, a former East African Railways 60 Class 4-8-2+2-8-4 Garratt, pauses for refreshment on its journey towards Voi with an overnight mixed freight from Moshi in Tanzania. Known colloquially as 'The Governors', the 60s were named after the British governors who at one time controlled Kenya, Uganda, and Tanganyika. This locomotive once bore the name *Sir James Hayes-Sadler* but this, along with all other such splendid-sounding names, was removed after the nations' independence.

The modern, thriving town of Karlovac, in Croatia, seems an unlikely location in which to find veteran locomotives dating back to the days of the Austro-Hungarian Empire, but several Yugoslav State Railway 51 Class 2-6-2Ts (above) are retained for working the lightly laid branch to Sisak. The section between Karlovac and Vrginmost was opened in 1907, and it is possible that these locomotives, with their eleven-tonne axle loadings, have worked the line since its inception. The heavy maintenance work on No. 51.028 (right) at Karlovac requires char deposits to be shovelled from her smoke box. She was built for the Croatian State Railways in 1926.

A shedman adds a round of coal to the firebox of Yugoslav State Railway's Class 20 No. 131 (above) as his mate shovels hot ashes from her smokebox (facing page). This engine is one of several class 20 locomotives which survive on the lightly laid cross-country line from Sid in Serbia to Bijeljina in Bosnia. Overleaf: a rare scene in Java, depicting two four-cylinder compound Mallets, both tender and tank varieties, on the Cibatu to Cikajang line. On the left is the Indonesian State Railways C50 Class 2-6-6-0 alongside a CC10 Class 2-6-6OT.

Facing page: the last survivors of Indian Railways' British-styled XB Class Pacifics ended their days working from Rajamundry shed in Andra Pradesh. They were diagrammed on passenger work over the secondary lines around the Godavri Delta. One of the last survivors stands in Rajamundry shed yard as the depot fitters attend to a WG Class 2-8-2. Notice the return crank for the outside Walschaerts' valve gear in the vice on the work bench. Right: coaling by mobile steam train, the preferred method at many Indian depots. Mechanical coaling towers are not used and the steam cranes, though relatively labour-intensive, are far easier than the traditional method of manual coaling with wicker baskets. Below: an Indian Railways CWD Class 2-8-2 simmers on the coaling road at Bandel Depot as a mobile crane, built in Leeds during World War 1, eases the one-ton bucket into position. As the crane's fireman applies a round of coal, two shed labourers shovel up the spilt pieces in the foreground.

Left: one of Anshan Iron and Steel Works' fleet of SY Class Industrial Mikado 2-8-2s awaits minor repairs outside the plant's repair shop, while (below) a China Railways JF Class Mikado 2-8-2 receives a round of oil in the depot yard at Datong. This scene reveals the extremely handsome lines of the JF, her American ancestry fully evident. It was this kind of 'Light Mike' that was prolific on so many of America's railroads three-quarters of a century ago. Overleaf: coaling, watering, fire-raking and sanding at Harbin's huge steam sheds. On the left, a JF Class smokily heads back to one of the large marshalling yards, while the QJ on the right prepares to return to the main line.

The world's last main line worked entirely by steam engines spans the 232 miles from the Paraguayan capital Asuncion to Encarnacion on the Argentinian border. The line is known grandly as the 'Ferrocarril Presidente Carlos Antonio Lopez', and exhibits a variety of engines, among which are fine period 2-6-2 tanks built by Hawthorn Leslie in Newcastle-upon-Tyne between 1910 and 1913. The class numbered six engines which were built in unsuperheated form with slide valves. Above: No. 5 at Encarnacion, waiting to push wagons onto the decks of a paddle steamer for conveyance over the River Parana to the connection with Argentina's standard gauge Urquiza Railway.

ON THE MAIN LINES

Few people under the age of forty appreciate the flamboyance of the great age of steam. The steam locomotive is generally regarded as belonging to the distant past, related to the Victorian era rather than the modern world. In the popular mind of today, the steam train was slow and dirty, albeit charming, and in the interests of true progress it was an inevitable casualty. Nothing could be further from the truth. As recently as forty years ago, before the age of the motorway and the juggernaut, railways were the principal form of transport and a large percentage of the world's main lines were worked by steam. In postwar Britain, before the road economy became established, some 20,000 steam locomotives formed a safe, properly co-ordinated and disciplined form of transport which moved the nation's freight with speed and efficiency and provided passenger journeys to virtually every corner of the island.

This flamboyance has been lost as the steam age has declined across the world. The survivors are now sedate plodders and, but for very rare exceptions, are only found on humble duties, generally eking out their time until more recent forms of motive power can be introduced. This belies the inherent ability of steam traction, for as long ago as the 1840s, speeds faster than a mile a minute were well authenticated on Brunel's seven foot gauges. Before the end of the century, the railway races from London to Scotland produced some incredible performances: trains reached Aberdeen from London in as little as eight-and-a-half hours. This scintillating part of railway history also produced the run by the LNWR Jumbo 2-4-0 number 792 *Hardwick,* which achieved an average speed of just over sixty-seven miles per hour over the 144 miles from Crewe to Carlisle.

Three figure speeds were reached soon after the turn of the century, when the Great Western Railway's 4-4-0 *City of Truro* made its epic run down Wellington Bank and reached 102.3 miles an hour, but the 1930s must surely be regarded as the finest decade for world steam performance, as these years saw the *Cheltenham Flyer* cover the seventy-seven miles from London Paddington to Swindon in fifty-six minutes – a feat that earned it the title 'The World's Fastest Train'. Even more impressive were the attainments of the streamlined locomotives of the Thirties; in America high-speed Atlantics on the Chicago Milwaukee St. Paul and Pacific Railroad worked the *Hiawatha Express* over its 431-mile run from Chicago to Milwaukee in 400 minutes, including intermediate stops. To achieve this, sustained speeds in excess of a hundred miles an hour were normal. It was during the streamlined era in Britain that the world's speed record for steam traction was attained by Nigel Gresley's LNER Pacific *Mallard,* which reached a speed of 126 miles an hour on the descent of Stoke Bank between Grantham and Peterborough.

The popular characterisation of a steam locomotive crawling along with a heavy goods train is also far from representative of the age. Heavy mineral trains were characteristically slow, but from the early years of this century, mixed commodity trains worked at speeds that would compare favourably with those achieved on the motorway trucking routes of today. It is hard to conceive a time when virtually every commodity was moved by rail, being coordinated on its journey through marshalling yards, which achieved a breathtaking rate of efficiency, or else travelling directly via such epic freight trains as the overnight Grimsby fish hauls, which had fish that had been landed at Grimsby in the afternoon on the fishmonger's slab in London the following morning. In those days, the famous four o'clock Scotch goods from King's Cross ran on passenger train timings and carried hundreds of tonnes of freight with a rapidity and ease unheard of in today's road-orientated society.

In these pages, the last epic fling of the steam locomotive age is remembered. In Britain, this occurred on the Southern Region of British Railways, as services from London (Waterloo) to Southampton, Bournemouth and Weymouth were exclusively handled by steam as recently as 1967. The stars of these dramas were Bulleid's rebuilt Pacifics, and during the final year regular speeds of a hundred miles an hour were attained by engine crews conscious that a tradition was coming to its close. In Europe, steam flamboyance lasted longer and went out in a blaze of glory in the German Democratic Republic in 1977, when the magnificent 01 Class Pacifics of 1925 ceased working the express runs between Berlin and Dresden. Until that year, the 103-mile journey was regularly covered at scheduled speeds in excess of sixty miles an hour with loads of up to 400 tonnes, reaching top speeds of ninety miles an hour.

Today, hardly anything survives of steam's gallant performances. Exceptions occurred until recently in India, where the stalwart WP Pacifics were diagrammed to work expresses which sometimes reached speeds of seventy miles an hour and had short bursts of mile-a-minute timings, and to a lesser degree in China, where the magnificent RM and SL Class Pacifics occasionally reached a mile a minute with their increasingly heavy trains. The steam locomotive was the workhorse of the Industrial Revolution and possessed all the stolid characteristics of the reliable carthorse, but it was also a greyhound. Its ability to produce such differing performances with consummate ease is yet another aspect of its allure.

The Prussian P8 Class 4-6-0 was one of the most celebrated models in locomotive history and played an important part in the Prussian State Railway's standardisation scheme. The first example appeared in 1906, and by the 1930s almost 4,000 were in operation. They were the first superheated 4-6-0s to appear and, in many respects, they set the trend for the introduction of other 4-6-0s throughout Europe. They survived into the 1970s. Left: a Prussian P8 at Horb, in the Black Forest. The German Class 44 three-cylinder 2-10-0 (above) was almost as celebrated as the P8; some 2,000 were built, and they saw service in many countries during and after World War II. A supremely successful design, the 44s were capable of hauling 2,000-tonne trains along level track at thirty-five miles an hour. One of their last haunts was the Mosel Valley route from Koblenz to Trier.

Britain's last steam-hauled expresses survived on the London Waterloo to Southampton, Bournemouth and Weymouth line until 1967. Top left: a rebuilt Merchant Navy Class Pacific No. 35007, *Aberdeen Commonwealth*, passes Worting junction, and (left) an ex Great Western Class 1600 0-6-0 pannier tank at Tyseley. Above: a former Great Western Class 4500 branch-line prairie tank, No. 4555, resting in the preserved Dart Valley Railway in Devon. Overleaf: an ex LNER A4 Class Pacific No. 4498, *Sir Nigel Gresley*, returns to Bournemouth Central in readiness for working an enthusiasts' special to London Waterloo.

Facing page: the daily mixed from Sisak to Karlovac storms away from Vrginmost behind a Yugoslav State Railway 51 Class 2-6-2T, originally built in 1915 for the Hungarian State Railways. Yugoslavia's 20 Class 2-6-0 Moguls were designed by Borsig of Berlin, who were noted for building locomotives of a distinctly British appearance. The 20s were originally created to further Germany's imperialist aims to dominate, with the aid of her Turkish allies, all the territories from Berlin to Baghdad. They were carefully designed to be capable of working in all conditions over the difficult routes through Turkey and onwards to Baghdad. Above: a Yugoslav 20 Class 2-6-0 Mogul, and (right) a Yugoslav State Railway 28 Class 0-10-0, one of the country's famous designs inherited from the Austrian Empire.

The lines radiating from Izmir, on Turkey's Aegean coast, have long been celebrated for their fascinating variety of locomotive types; for example, a former Ottoman Railway 2-8-2 (above), built at Robert Stephenson's works in Newcastle-upon-Tyne, draws a mixed train along the line to Denizli. Right: a suburban train toils the heavy grades away from Izmir behind a 2-8-0, built in 1912 by Humboldt of Paris. Among Turkey's surviving steam fleet are some German Kriegslokomotives which date from World War II. The light axle loading of these trains allows them to work a wide variety of routes. They are regarded as mixed-traffic engines, working both passenger and freight duties, as well as mixed trains. The Kriegslokomotive engine shown leaving Egridir (overleaf) was built by the Maschinenbau und Bahnbedarf AG of Berlin at the height of the war in 1943.

These pictures of Poland's fabulous high-stepping PT47 Class Mikado 2-8-2s (these pages and overleaf) were taken at a line-side base near Kamieniec in the summer of 1983. These engines were responsible for some of the last express passenger duties in Europe; they have large-diameter driving wheels and the sleek characteristics of a Pacific, but as Mikados they pull away more quickly from station stops and climb gradients with more ease. The class numbered 180 examples, built between the late 1940s and early 1950s by the Polish builders Cegielski and Chrzanòw, and are descended from a 1920s design. The PT47s are important historically in being the finest surviving examples of the Polish school of locomotive design, which flowered after the First World War when Poland emerged as a united and self-governing country.

In a world in which the steam engine is relegated to relatively menial duties, the striking sights on China Railways' main lines, where an army of 4,500 QJ Class engines perform their arduous duties, are hard to believe. Above: a QJ Class 2-10-2 storms Wang Gang Bank south of Harbin with a train loaded with wood from the forests of the northeast, and (top right) a QJ heads southwards from Anshan along the main line to Dalian, with Saddle Mountain in the background. On the same journey, another QJ (right) heads for the port at Dalian in winter, towing an oil train. The contrast between exhaust effects, caused by the differences in winter and summer air, are marked. Overleaf: a QJ running wrong line, slides down the bank into Anshan with a heavy freight from the Port of Dalian, on the Yellow Sea coast.

Above: America's S160 class Austerities were known as 'GIs'. Over 2,000 were built, and their wide postwar dispersal rendered them as one of the all-time greats in world locomotive history.
Facing page: a train of empties heads back along Brazil's Teresa Cristina Railway main line behind a Baldwin 2-8-2 of 1946. Known as 'Grimy Hog', this engine originally worked on Brazil's metre-gauge Centro Oeste network. 'Hog' is a typical American product, scaled down for metre-gauge operation.

Above: a French Railways 141R Class 2-8-2 heads away from Rang du Fliers with a southbound semi-fast. These engines were supplied to France as emergency aid following the ravages of the Second World War, when the country's total of 17,000 locomotives was reduced to 3,000. Known as the 'Liberations,' the first one was steamed at Lima's works in July, 1945, having been designed by Baldwin. Ultimately totalling 1,340 locomotives, this simple, rugged class contrasted enormously with traditional French engines, but they were popular and provided an ideal mixed-traffic type which survived until the very end of steam traction on French Railways. Left: a South African Railways 23 Class 4-8-2 climbs the 1 in 100 bank to the north of Bloemfontein with an express passenger train for Froonstad.
Facing page: one of India's celebrated metre-gauge MacArthur WD Class 2-8-2s bursts away from Gorakhpur with a stopping passenger train. She is No. 1651, built for the United States Army Transportation Corps by Davenport of Iowa in 1944.

These pages: Sankong Bridge in Harbin, possibly the finest train-watching place left in the world. It is no exaggeration to say that on busy days a steam train passes beneath this bridge every three minutes. Activities centre around the JF Class 2-8-2s, traditionally assigned to yard transfers and hump shunting, and the magnificent departures of the double-headed QJ-hauled freights heading southwards along the main line through Manchuria. Amid the multifarious sounds of the trains and shunting activities comes the ringing voice of the yard controller as he directs operations. The right-hand track is the lower section of the hump used for assembling the southbound trains, while on the far left is seen the lower section of the hump for assembling northbound freights from Harbin. Sankong, similar to many yards throughout China, represents the proper use of railroads. As such, it is reminiscent of yards once seem across America before the advent of a road- and air-based economy. Overleaf: a pair of Vulcan Ironwork's decapods draws a heavy train out of the yards at Irmak. American steam superpower on Turkish Railways survived into the 1980s on the busy, steeply graded line from Irmak up to the Black Sea town of Zonguldak

Left: this handsome Mikado is one of the Turkish State Railways' 46201 Class and is seen shunting at Irmak. She is one of a class of fifty-three engines built by Baldwin, Lima and Alco for the War Department to see service with the Middle East Forces. Some went directly to Turkey during the war, to be followed by later batches from Iraq during the mid Fifties. Above: one of the world's last Texas type 2-10-4s speeds a string of empties along Brazil's Teresa Cristina Railway – an example of American steam superpower scaled down to metre-gauge operation.

The beauty of Portugal's Douro Valley makes a perfect setting for an inside cylinder 4-6-0 (above) easing a freight train into Ferradosa, en-route to Barca d'Alva on the Spanish frontier. These 5ft 6in gauge period pieces are among the most handsome locomotives in Europe and were part of a class of six engines delivered in 1910 from Henschel of Germany for the Portuguese State Railways.

The status of steam traction around the world is directly related to national affluence. Predictably, the first countries to eradicate steam were the USA and Canada, followed closely by Scandinavia and Western Europe, where steam traction is rapidly heading for extinction. The Western economies are all closely related in terms of social, technical and economic development, so in the related economies of Japan, Australia and New Zealand, the steam age has also passed into history. A very different situation applies in the developing world. Here societies are necessarily more disparate, not technically inter-related and, with the massive social problems in these lands, 'make do and mend' is the over-riding philosophy.

In France, steam has all but vanished and yet, within the last twenty years, four-cylinder Pacifics were working up to Calais with international trains and the 141R Class Mikados, supplied by American builders as aid to France's devastated railways following the ravages of World War II, could be found in many parts of the country. Even a few work-weary 140C Class 2-8-0s dating back to World War I remained active around the old battlefield regions of Verdun.

West German mainline steam survived into the 1970s with 2-10-0s, 2-8-2s and Pacifics – all German standard designs of the 1920s – active in various parts of the country, but especially on the busy line from Rheine to Emden. Another famous route was the scenic line through the Mosel Valley from Koblenz to Trier, which reverberated with the roar of three-cylinder 2-10-0s of 1920s vintage hauling trains in excess of 1,500 tonnes.

Steam lasted even longer on the Iberian Peninsula, and with a far greater diversity of types and gauges. During the early 1960s Spain had one of the most varied and antiquated locomotive fleets on earth; although the main lines were standardised at 5ft 6in, at least five other gauges could be found in use on secondary railways throughout the country. The boom in foreign tourism that began in the late Fifties transformed Spain's economy, and a lot of the money earned was used to modernise the railways, resulting in many of the antiquities vanishing within a few short years. The dawn of the Seventies, though, still found the country running massive 4-8-0s, 4-8-2s and 2-8-2s and a sprinkling of older types on shunting and trip work. The extensive coal-mining areas of the northwest remained havens for innumerable veterans; a handful survive today, though others lie derelict.

Neighbouring Portugal's main lines were also built to a 5ft 6in gauge, and services on the scenic Douro Valley route, which ran from Oporto on the Atlantic coast to Barca d'Alva on the Spanish frontier, was a haven for the world's last inside cylinder 4-6-0s. Portugal also had a large network of metre gauge secondary lines, some of which fed into the Douro Valley and sported 2-4-6-0 Mallets with copper-capped chimneys and gleaming brasswork.

Even more exciting were the metre gauge suburban services around Oporto, as here was a varied fleet of copper-capped antiquities in service on an intensively used network. With smoke-filled tunnels, vintage coaching stock and shrieking, panting locomotives, these services represented the last fling of the classic Victorian suburban railway.

Italy also ran a fine fleet of vintage locomotives, all based around a series of standard designs which evolved as long ago as 1905, when the country's railways were nationalised. Ostensibly, these were all out of use by the early 1980s, but, as isolated steam workings can still be found, the true situation remains an enigma.

In Scandinavia, Norway and Sweden were only a few years behind the USA in declaring against steam traction, although in Finland it survived much longer and the early Seventies saw a fine fleet of locomotives comprised of 2-8-0s, 2-8-2s and Pacifics. Even when these were replaced, many were mothballed in strategic reserves around the country. During the intervening years, some of these have been broken up and others purchased for preservation, but large numbers still remain on abandoned lines in forested areas.

The traveller in search of working steam in Western Europe today will find little to satisfy him, although industrial lines still yield some delightful discoveries. Odd survivors exist in Germany, where Fireless locomotives can also be found in a variety of industrial locations. The Fireless also lingers on in Austria, but the high spot of Western Europe must be Switzerland, where the SLM works recently contracted to build three new steam locomotives for one of the country's narrow gauge lines.

In the Warsaw Pact countries of centralised economies, labour and fuel costs are equated on a different scale and railways remain pre-eminent over road transportation. In these countries, a general abundance of coal and a lack of oil ensured that steam not only survived, but remained free from commercial pressures for change. The result was that steam traction survived much longer behind the Iron Curtain and 0149 Class 2-6-2s can still be found in active mainline service in Poland, as can German Kriegslokomotive 2-10-0s and the fabulous passenger hauling PT47 Class 2-8-2 Mikados. In the former German Democratic Republic, Krieglokomotives still appear on the odd secondary line, although this country is now more revered for its narrow gauge systems, which, though slowly declining, still sport a fascinating variety of designs on delightfully rural systems.

Hewn from the territorial carve-up of the Austro-Hungarian Empire following World War I, Yugoslavia is a land of great territorial complexity. Its locomotive history reflects this; the country was, until recent years, host to one of the most varied and fascinating motive power fleets on earth. Here, classics of Austrian, Hungarian, and Serbian design mixed with the standard types ultimately created for Yugoslavia proper, while added to these was a wide variety of war designs, many of which came in the form of reparations from both the world wars. Although much of the complexity has been swept away in recent years, it is still possible to see Serbian Moguls working turn and turn about with Hungarian 2-6-2 tanks of early twentieth-century origin, and contrasting with such classic wartime designs as the United States Army Transportation Corps 0-6-0Ts of World War II. In the former Yugoslavia, industrial lines are havens for a few rare and obsolete types, but these – in common with the railways of the former Warsaw Pact countries – are generally hazardous to visit, or else inaccessible.

Above: *El Elsa*, the veteran Sharp Stewart 0-6-0T at Sabero colliery in northern Spain, emerges from a tunnel with a coal train bound for the RENFE exchange.

Above: simmering gently in Portugal's Oporto Trindade station is a 0-4-4-0T Mallet built in 1908. Overleaf left: the ultimate Spanish locomotives were the mighty 4-8-4 Confederations, ten of which were built by Maquinista of Barcelona during the mid 1950s. Overleaf right: though hastily built by America to help restore France's railroads following World War II, the 141R Class Mikados proved to be brilliant locomotives.

The 4-8-0 type was widely used in Spain, where weight restrictions and curves abounded on many lines. Shown (above) is one of these engines boiling up at Salamanca. Facing page: one of the Portuguese Railway's magnificent four-cylinder compound 2-8-0s, first introduced in 1912, at work on the Douro Valley line.

The 740 Class 2-8-0 was a standard freight design on Italian Railways for some sixty years and was the country's most numerous class. They survived until the end of regular steam working, and even today one hears occasional reports of 740s being turned out for pilot and ballasting work. Left: a 740 passing through Cornuda with a Belluno-Treviso freight. The 740 Class was one of the types chosen by Italian Railways to be rebuilt with Crosti boilers. This marvellous innovation was a preheater drum slung beneath the normal boiler to convey the hot gases from the smokebox in order to heat the feed water. This resulted in the chimney being placed at the firebox end of the locomotive. The modified engines were reclassified 741, and some eighty examples were so modified during the 1950s. Above: a 741 drawing a passenger train along the Fortessa to San Candido line in the northern part of the country.

In the early '70s, Italy operated about 1,000 steam locomotives. Most were standard classes whose origin could be traced back to the nationalisation of Italy's railways in 1905. One of the stalwart designs to emerge was the 625 Class 2-6-0 Mogul (these pages). They were typically Italian in appearance, with a delightful vintage look, and were to be found on many secondary lines across the country until the end of regular steam working.

The 50 Class 2-10-0 (facing page) was one of the principal designs used on German Railways. It first appeared in 1938 and over 3,000 were constructed, forming the basis for the German Kriegslokomotive of World War II. Over 6,000 were ultimately built, making the basic design of the mixed traffic 2-10-0 one of the leading locomotive types in world history. Above: an Austrian State Railway narrow-gauge 298 Class crosses the viaduct at Waldrenkirchen, on the Garsten to Molln line.

The 25-kilometre-long Selketalbahn runs amid the scenic beauty of the Harz Mountains and is possibly the most delightful of all the German Democractic Republic's narrow-gauge lines. Built to a gauge of one metre, it is traversed by the last Mallets working in the country; they are 0-4-4-Ts and date from the early years of the century. The line begins at Gernrode and runs to a junction at Alexisbad, where it splits; one section climbing up to Harzgerode and the other heading through lush meadowland to Strassberg. Above and right: 0-4-4-Ts departing from Gernrode early in the morning and heading through the flower-strewn countryside with trains bound for Alexisbad.

Above: two of the exhibits at the narrow-gauge railway museum at Wenecja, in Poland. The engine on the right is of tremendous historical significance: it was the forerunner of the famous Feldbahn engines of World War I, having been built by Orenstein and Koppel in 1911. Right: the last surviving Feldbahn 0-8-0T on the forestry system at Czarna Bialystok, alongside the Russian border in northeastern Poland. Several thousand Feldbahns were built to follow the German armies all over Europe during the First World War. After the war they were surplus to military requirements and many gravitated to forestry and industrial railways.

Left: two classic European designs boil up side by side in Slovenia. On the left is one of the German Kriegslokomotive 2-10-0s, some of which passed to Yugoslavia as reparations following World War II, and on the right a 28 Class Austrian State Railway 0-10-0, many of which were ceded to Yugoslavia upon its creation as a separate nation following World War I. One of the largest and most important of the Hungarian State Railway designs was the 424 Class 4-8-0 (above). This type also saw prolific service in Yugoslavia, for whom examples were built in Budapest until the mid 1950s. They formed the Yugoslav State Railway's 11 Class.

Watching these magnificent 0-10-0s (these pages) working over the hill lines of Slovenia with their heavy freights was a memorable experience. The type is descended from the 180 Class two-cylinder compound 0-10-0s of 1900, designed by the legendary Austrian engineer Karl Golsdorf. When rebuilt as simples with superheaters, they were reclassified 80.9 and the type performed magnificently on the sinuous routes throughout Austria. On the Yugoslav State Railway they were known as the 28 Class. Above: one of them prepares to take water at Stanjel, a village of Roman origin, whilst heading a Nova Gorica to Sezana freight. The locomotive dates from the Austrian Empire, and the track was cast by Krupp of Germany during the 19th century. Right: a Yugoslav State Railway 51 Class 2-6-2T heads a morning freight from Karlovac to Sisak.

Yugoslavia's 51 Class 2-6-2Ts (these pages) represent one of the most remarkable survivors in Europe. Originally the Hungarian State Railway Class 375, the first examples of the 51 Class appeared in 1907. They were important among several branch line types designed for the lightly laid rural lines of the territory and, despite their archaic appearance, they continued to be built in Hungary until 1959. Fifteen were built at Yugoslavia's Slavonksi Brod works in 1942. The stud currently active on the Karlovac to Sisak line includes both original Hungarian and Yugoslavian engines. Above: the overnight passenger train from Karlovac to Sisak during its long wait at Vrginmost.

Turkey has achieved much recognition over the last decade for retaining a wide variety of standard gauge designs descended from German, British and American builders. The Turkish State Railways have been intent upon dieselisation for many years, but have never been able to implement the programme as scheduled and to this day, an ever dwindling variety of steam designs can still be found in the country. Top left: a fine contrast in motive power at the EKI colliery exchange sidings in Catalagzi, in Zonguldak on the Black Sea coast. On the left is a former Turkish Railways 0-6-0T, which now belongs to the colliery for shunting the exchange sidings. On the right is one of the colliery's metre-gauge 0-6-0 pannier tanks, built by Bagnalls of Stafford in 1942. The two shed pilots (left) at Irmak junction are highly distinctive designs. On the left is an ex Prussian G82 Class 2-8-0 and on the right, one of the celebrated Stanier 8F 2-8-0s which passed to Turkey following World War II. Above: a magnificently trimmed example of a Turkish State Railway German Kriegslokomotive, complete with the Turkish state emblem on its cab side.

This powerful Turkish Railways two-cylinder 2-8-0 (above) was built to the design of the Prussian G82 Class, which once numbered more than 1,000 locomotives – sixty-two being built for Turkey alone between 1927-35. The former LMS Stanier 8F Class 2-8-0 (facing page) was one of Britain's most numerous steam types, of which over 700 examples were built. Many were built during World War II, and twenty examples eventually passed to Turkey, where survivors lingered on, performing secondary duties until well into the 1980s. Overleaf: dawn on the border of the Arctic Circle during a footplate journey on Finnish Railway's TR1 Class 2-8-2 Mikado No. 1074. The engine was working a Rovaniemi to Raajarvi ballast haul and, during the course of the journey, crossed the Arctic Circle into Finnish Lapland.

Finland's highly distinctive designs were among the bright spots in the closing years of steam in Europe and Scandinavia. One of the best-loved designs were the TK3 Class 2-8-0s. The Finns called them 'Little Jumbos', and with an axle loading of only 10.7 tonnes, they were able to work over a wide variety of lines. First introduced in 1927, building continued until 1953, by which time a total of 161 had been constructed, making them Finland's most numerous type. Many were wood burners and were supplied with characteristic spark-arresting chimneys, such as the one on No. 1163 (above) engaged in tripping duties around Rovaniemi. Along with many countries, Finland adopted a standardisation policy based around Mikado 2-8-2s and Pacific 4-6-2s with interchangable boilers. Right: one of their TR1 Class Mikados, which totalled sixty-seven engines. Known as 'Ristos', they were among the last steam locomotives to work in Finland, and many have been mothballed as part of a strategic reserve. Overleaf: as winter relaxes its icy grip upon Finland's rivers, a TV1 Class 2-8-0 ambles towards Kontiomäki with a sand ballast train for permanent way engineers. Introduced in 1917, the TV1 totalled ninety-seven engines when building finished in 1945.

STEAM IN INDIA AND PAKISTAN

Running some 750 locomotives, the Indian subcontinent is now the world's second largest bastion of steam traction. With 7,000 examples in service, China is well ahead of this, but their fleet is standardised, containing few locomotives more than fifty years old, whereas the surviving engines on the Indian sub-continent are highly varied and often of great antiquity.

The vastness of Indian railways is hard to appreciate by European standards. In addition to the great distances covered, the network is densely laid and intensively utilised. Roads, such as those known in the West, barely exist, so the railway remains the preferred form of transportation. The building of India's railways was one of the great achievements of the British Empire; most of the extensive system was laid before the end of the Raj, having been financed, designed, engineered, built and operated under British jurisdiction. The railways constructed by those intrepid pioneers extended from Burma to the Khyber Pass and from the Himalayas to Ceylon. The railway unified India industrially and socially, just as the English language unified her culturally. Four gauges eventually came into operation and these created mainline networks of five foot, six inches and metre gauge, alongside many feeder systems and rural railways that adopted a gauge of 2ft, or 2ft 6in.

Imperial locomotive designs for the Indian railways followed those of the old country; indeed, the subcontinent's railways, as they evolved in all their private diversity, resembled the pre-grouping years of Britain's railways. During the nineteenth century, the companies ordered their designs with predictable individualism from Britain, though the building of locomotives in the purest of British traditions had begun at Jamalpur and Ajmer before the turn of the century.

This proliferation of types caused concern, so, in 1905, the British Engineering Standards Association (BESA) designs were prepared. These were intended to fulfil the needs of all the subcontinent's 5ft 6in gauge lines and were comprised of exactly the kind of locomotive then prevalent in Britain:. inside-cylinder 0-6-0s, inside-cylinder 4-6-0s, Atlantics, 4-6-0s and 2-8-0s. The BESA standards were exported in large numbers from many of the major British builders and fulfilled their task superbly, but by the 1920s loads were increasing and the narrow fireboxes of the traditional British locomotives were causing increasing difficulties with the poorer standard Indian coal. This led to the next major series of British designs for the subcontinent – the famous X series. These were comprised of three classes of Pacific for light, medium and heavy work, classified XA, XB and XC, and two Mikado 2-8-2s for medium and heavy freight hauls, classified XD and XE respectively. All these classes had wide fire boxes designed to cope with poorer coal, and the series was rounded off by the heavy shunting XF and mighty hump-shunting XG, so necessary for the vast marshalling yards that had grown to keep pace with Indian railway development.

With their wide fireboxes (a design concept derived from America), the X series represented a partial departure from traditional British practice, and the departure was completed during World War II when India took a number of pure American designs, one of which was a 5ft 6in gauge version of the classic S160 2-8-0 supplied by America as aid for Britain and Europe. America also provided the AWE and CWD Class Mikados, which were pure American versions of the XE and XD types. The ruggedness of these bar-framed imports proved ideal for Indian conditions, and thenceforth the subcontinent looked to American traditions for the remainder of her major steam designs. This was made all the easier after 1947 when British rule ceased. India's final choice of broad gauge standards was restricted to two classes: a highly Americanised and partly streamlined Pacific classified WP, which first appeared in 1947, and a closely related Mikado classified WG for heavy freight work ,which first appeared in 1950. These designs were built in many countries and, in all, reached a total of more than 3,000 engines.

The world-famous Indian variety of engines does not apply to those designed for broad gauge. None of the BESA standards or even the X series remain in line service, although isolated examples from both groups may be found on industrial lines. Even the American incursions from the Second World War have recently been taken out of service, which left the entire broad gauge network with only WLs, WPs and WGs. Broad-gauge steam on India's main lines has now been phased out. At the end of their days both could be found performing the duties for which they were originally designed, although WPs are increasingly found on secondary stopping trains (jobs which are so low key in performance that they are easily interchangeable with WGs), whilst now WGs are usually relegated to shunting and tripping work.

The varied collection of classic British designs for the metre gauge has also disappeared and services on these networks are now dominated by the YP Pacifics and YG Mikados – the American-influenced counterparts of the WPs and WGs. A little variety exists on the narrow gauge lines that are not interconnected, which tend to retain their original form of individualistic motive power wherever steam traction survives. The most famous of these is the Darjeeling and Himalayan Railway, which climbs 7,407 feet to the former British summer resort boasting commanding views of the snow-capped Himalayas. The charm and rusticity of these systems is unequalled anywhere in the world and eloquently mirrors the heyday of the rural railway in Britain; here copper-capped antiquities whose spiritual home lies in the soft English countryside still play a vital role in the rural economy of developing India.

Right: a British-built inside cylinder 0-6-0 from the BESA period approaches Dandot, in the Pakistan Punjab. Similar engines were used on the 5ft 6in gauge lines of the Indian subcontinent, from the Khyber Pass to Bangladesh.

A great variety of types is also to be found on India's industrial lines, and many of these are ex-mainliners, including some ninetheeth-century examples from small, regionally based systems dating back to the very beginning of railway development in India. A perfect example is the once ubiquitous F Class 0-6-0; this locomotive was built in vast numbers as a metre gauge standard design from the 1870s until the 1920s, and is recognised today as one of the classics of world locomotive history.

In absolute contrast, neighbouring Pakistan has relatively few narrow gauge lines and a somewhat limited metre gauge system. It is the country's 5ft 6in gauge lines that have bought it world renown, as here two of the most important types in the BESA standard series – amazingly and against all odds – remain hard at work. These are the inside cylinder 0-6-0 and related inside cylinder 4-4-0 – the definitive freight and express passenger types of late-Victorian Britain.

The two principal forms of British locomotive during the late 19th century were the inside cylinder 0-6-0, for heavy freight and mixed traffic duties, and the closely related inside cylinder 4-4-0, for express passenger duties. Most of Britain's privately owned railway companies possessed both types, often fitted with interchangeable boilers. During these years there were enormous exports of locomotives to British India, and almost identical designs were prepared for the subcontinent under the BESA scheme at the beginning of the 20th century. It is incredible that today, more than eighty years later, examples of these definitive Victorian 0-6-0s and 4-4-0s remain in evidence on the railways of Pakistan. The principal centre is the cross-country junction of Malakal, in the Punjab. All are now oil-burning, since Pakistan has no coal fields. Left: an inside cylinder 0-6-0 heads away from Malakal as a gracefully-shaped inside cylinder 4-4-0 (above) boils up in the depot yard.

Many British classics were exported to India under the X series standardisation scheme of the 1920s, notably the beautiful XC Class Pacific (above), and the XD Class 2-8-2 Mikado (right). The XCs have a typical 1920s appearance and were the last greyhounds of British steam to remain in world service. The class totalled seventy-two engines, which came primarily from the Vulcan Foundry at Newton-le-Willows in Lancashire, although the final twelve came from the legendary Clyde shipbuilding firm of Beardsmore during the early '30s. The XD Class 2-8-2 Mikado was a powerful heavy freight and mixed traffic design, first introduced from the Vulcan Foundry in 1927. When building finished in 1948, the class totalled almost 200 engines. They were well regarded, bearing, as they did, all the elements of traditional British craftsmanship. XDs were operating 1,800-tonne trains over the seventy-seven miles from Dornakal Junction to Vijaywada until the 1960s, completing the journey in two-and-a-quarter hours – enduring proof that the steam locomotive is not an outmoded relic. Overleaf: HSM Class 2-8-0 No. 26190 takes us back to the BESA period. She was built for the Bengal and Nagpur Railway by Armstrong Whitworth of Newcastle-upon-Tyne in 1924. These handsome British 2-8-0s ended their days working empty stock trains around Calcutta.

For many years, railway operations around Calcutta's vast docks were performed by these heavy duty 0-6-2 side tanks (left and top left), which first came from Hunslet's Leeds works in 1945. Having found the type satisfactory, the Calcutta Port Trust – unlike most industrial steam users – decided to standardise its locomotive fleet around one design. Accordingly, when further locomotives were needed, the Calcutta Port Trust insisted on the same design. That notwithstanding, the second batch came from Henschel of Germany, and the final batch from Mitsubishi of Japan in 1954. Above: an Indian Iron and Steel Corporation Andrew Barclay built 0-4-2T heads a loaded iron-ore train to the South Eastern Railway's connection at Manoharpur.

Facing page: a 0-6-4T, built by Bagnalls of Stafford in 1914, on the 2ft 6in gauge line from Burdwan to Katwa. Above: the world-famous Darjeeling-Himalayan Railway, which climbs 7,400 feet during its fifty-five mile journey to the former British summer resort. Overleaf: one of the last surviving Indian Railway XD Class 2-8-2s.

The British sailed from Calcutta in Scottish-built paddle steamers and plied their way up the rivers of what is now Bangladesh to enter the great Brahmaputra River, from there to sail eastwards and enter the dense, inhospitable and leech-ridden jungles of Assam. Once there, the intrepid pioneers developed many industries: logging, tea planting and coal mining. It was perhaps inevitable that Staffordshire-built saddle tanks should follow their enterprise and today, almost a century later, some still survive. *David* (above) worked at Tirap colliery close to the Burmese border, coming originally from Bagnall's Castle Engine Works in Stafford in 1924. Left: *Sally*, a Bagnall engine of 1930. These engines were supplied to the Assam Railways and Trading Company, the organisation established by the British to develop the wealth of Upper Assam. The 0-6-0 crane tank (facing page) was exported from Manning Wardle's works in Leeds in 1903. Her crane structure and the auxiliary engine which drives it came from Joseph Booth and Sons, who were located in the Leeds suburb of Rodley. She worked at an Indian sleeper depot and part of her duty was to lift tree trunks and convey them to the sawmill to be cut into sleeper lengths for use on Indian Railway's main lines.

A pair of Fireless engines (top left) work at the Ludlow Jute Mill on the banks of the Hooghley River, Calcutta. They are both 0-4-0s from Orenstein and Koppel, but of very different design. Both have their feed valves located at the front, but the engine on the left has its cylinders and chimney to the rear, whilst the right-hand engine has conventionally-placed cylinders and chimney. The veteran 0-4-2 well tank (left) is possibly the last survivor from Dick Kerr's Britannia works in Kilmarnock, Scotland. She was originally built for the Karachi Port Trust, but ended her days working at the Dhilwan creosoting plant in India's Punjab. Above: *Cheetal*, a delightful 0-6-0 well tank built by John Fowler's works, Leeds, in 1923, heads along the 2ft gauge metals of the Upper India Sugar Mills with a loaded train. Overleaf: one of Ludlow Jute Mills' Fireless engines, having taken a fresh charge of steam from the factory boilers, eases along the jetty with a loaded train.

Left: an Indian Railways WP Class Pacific 4-6-2, one of the home-built examples from Chittaranjan Locomotive Works in West Bengal. The first examples were delivered from Baldwin in 1947 and when building finished twenty years later, the class totalled 755 examples. Below: three Indian Railways AWC Class 2-8-0s, 5ft 6in gauge versions of the classic standard-gauge S160s of World War II. They numbered sixty engines, all of which came from Baldwin in 1944 and some of which survived until the late 1970s, the last examples being allocated to Naihati Depot in Bengal, where they were employed on shunting and tripping duties.

These pages: Indian Railways' WP Class Pacific No. 7247, whose appearance indicates the tremendous care and attention devoted to the annual locomotive beauty competitions. Indian locomotives, in all their diversity, are perhaps the most decorated among the world's surviving steam fleets, but this example, as turned out by Asansol shed, has had countless hours of loving care bestowed upon her. No. 7247 was one of 220 WPs delivered to India in 1949 from Baldwin and the Montreal Locomotive Works in Canada.

STEAM IN CHINA

Over recent years China has received international fame for her steam railways. The media throughout the Western world has reported the fact that China continues to build steam locomotives – news which amazed enthusiasts and laymen alike. With 7,000 steam locomotives in service, China is now synonymous with the age of steam. The country is vast, contains one quarter of the world's population and has become a powerful, industrialised nation largely dependent upon public transport. Given this situation, it is not difficult to imagine the density of operations throughout China's enormous railway network.

Before China's opening up to the West, it was popularly believed that the country was host to all kinds of exotic rarities, but the opposite proved to be the case. Standardisation has been rigorously pursued, both before and especially since the founding of the People's Republic – only Russia has ever approached such a remarkable degree of standardisation. Of the 7,000 locomotives at work, some 6,000 can be accounted for by three basic types. Topping the list are the QJ Class Advanced Forward 2-10-2s, with over 3,000 believed to be in service. These handle the heaviest freightwork, aided by the smaller JS Class construction 2-8-2s of which there are some 1,500 in service. The JSs are based on an earlier, Mikado-classified JF of which around 200 remain at work, whilst slightly smaller is the SY Class Aiming High Industrial Mikado with another 1,800 in service. Only two passenger classes survived in recent years, both Pacifics: the SL6, which dates back to the 1930s, and the more recent RM Class.

Though heavily standardised, China's railways present the enthusiast with incomparable spectacles. Nowhere else can busy main lines be found which are almost a hundred percent steam operated on which trains pass every twenty minutes or so day and night. A typical line may see QJs on the long-distance freights, a few JSs on pick-up freights, and perhaps one of the Pacific classes on certain passenger turns, although other equally busy lines may only see QJs. The density of activity and full-blooded action more than offsets the lack of variety, but, in any case, the locomotives within any given class vary greatly, if not in mechanical details, then in terms of embellishments, which in China take on a fascinating diversity and provide a constant source of interest.

In view of the massive world publicity about China's steam railways, it is sometimes supposed that the country has an outright steam policy, but many main lines are electrified and this form of traction proceeds apace as, indeed, does dieselisation. Many of China's long-distance express trains were dieselised years ago and the remainder have now been converted, partly because the increasingly heavy weights are beyond the capacity of the Pacifics. Despite China's avid modernisation programme, the steam total has fluctuated remarkably little. This is a unique situation brought about by two basic factors. The first stems from the fact that the country's economy is developing rapidly, leading to a massive increase in rail traffic – new locomotives merely cope with the increase instead of eroding the steam total. The second factor is that China continues to build new railways, many of them important long-distant routes, and as these tend to use modern traction from the outset, they are another area of demand for all the diesels and electrics that China can either build or import. Equally important, though, is the fact that when some of the non-standard and even older examples of the standard classes are withdrawn, they have been replaced by newly built examples of classes QJ, JS and SY.

Throughout history, the Chinese have been attributed with great wisdom and certainly their policy of utilising whatever form of traction is most appropriate for a particular circumstance has been refreshingly clear in its thinking. The country is rich in coal and iron reserves and also has an abundance of labour. Given these factors in a centralised socialist economy, it makes good sense to use steam traction.

So vast and exciting are China's main lines that many of the country's industrial and narrow gauge systems have tended to be overlooked. In the case of collieries and iron and steel works, the standard SY Mikado has now all but replaced the fascinating array of former mainline types that survived in these environments until recent years, but the narrow gauge systems see a completely different range of motive power, although even here standardisation is remarkably advanced. Of the country's forestry lines, 762 millimetre gauge 0-8-0s, built to a basic standard design, predominate over many systems, particularly in the northeastern province of Heilongjiang. Descended from a Russian engine, isolated examples of this type continue to be built at the Harbin Forest Machinery Company's works. Far more extensive than these systems, however, are China's local railways; these are also built to 762 millimetre gauge and operated by provincial or local governments to provide public passenger and freight services in rural areas. In Henan and Hebei provinces alone, these local railways have 1,550 miles of route in operation. Many are worked by steam, although diesels are encroaching, but whatever form of motive power is used, it has recently been reported that the average cost per route mile of these local lines is between a third and a half of the cost of road transport. As with China's burgeoning main lines, construction of local railways continues and it is anticipated that by the end of the century some 10,000 route miles could be in operation.

So China is the country of steam, but equally importantly and perhaps more accurately, she is the country of railways – perhaps the last truly railway-based economy on earth. One fears that as Western commerical influences exert ever greater pressures on China as part of her opening-up policy, this situation may change and the idea of road development begin to take hold. However, if this does happen, it will be a long way into the future; for the time being, China's railways still fulfil their purpose throughout the nation, and in so doing provide a stable and secure base for steam traction into the forseeable future.

Facing page: on a misty morning at Harbin, in winter temperatures of -35°C, a QJ Class 2-10-2 pulls up to the water column during routine servicing.

The pride of Harbin was QJ Class 2-10-2 No. 2470 *Zhou De* (these pages). She was one of the best-kept locomotives on China Railways and was a Harbin engine for many years. Zhou De was one of China's ten marshalls and the man who led the Red Army from its formation in 1927 through the revolution of 1949, when he was second only to Mao himself. Before the founding of the People's Republic of China in 1949, the Red Army was known as the 'Zhou De Mao Army.' Above: with its mechanical stoker activated, *Zhou De* approaches the summit of Wang Gang Bank at the head of a heavy southbound freight. Right: General Zhou De stares impassively from the smokebox of QJ Class No. 2470 as she waits to leave Sankong yard in Harbin. Overleaf: a long rake of mineral wagons heads southwards from Anshan behind a QJ Class 2-10-2 bound for the Yellow Sea port of Daliam.

Harbin is known as China's coldest city. The biting Manchurian wind blows in vicious, stinging blasts in temperatures so low that it is almost impossible to control a camera. A pair of QJs (facing page) receive the all clear from Sankong yard and, with chime whistles ringing and mechanical stokers activated, they ease their 2,000-tonne wood train forward. Above: two QJ Class 2-10-2s make a vigorous assault on Wang Gang Bank at the head of a half-mile-long southbound freight. Right: the amplified voice of the yard controller directing operations at Sankong is momentarily drowned by the departure of two QJs with a heavy southbound freight. Overleaf: the big freeze of the Manchurian winter is so severe that it deposits thick layers of ice on all but the very hottest parts of the locomotives.

The YJ Class industrial 2-6-2 Prairie (left) clearly reveals her American ancestry. The YJs are descended from, and almost identical to, the earlier PL2 Class, first introduced in 1941. The JF was for many years a principal freight hauler on many of China's main lines but, with the advent of the JS and QJ classes, they were relegated to secondary work, primarily shunting, tripping and freight-transfer work between marshalling yards. Engine No. 2422 (above) has for many years been the shed pilot at Changchun. She is immediately recognisable by her tender, cut down to facilitate movement of dead engines onto the turntable and into the various bays of the semi-round house. Overleaf: the magic of the steam age captured in a glorious view of the Sangkong yard.

Left: fitters at Changchun shed in Manchuria focus their attention on Tangshan-built Industrial SY Class Mikado 2-8-2 No. 1368. Since SYs are exclusively an industrial design, it is unusual to find them at mainline depots, but it is possible that the engine had come to Changchun for specialized attention from an industrial establishment in the vicinity. Below: PL2 Class Prairie 2-6-2 No. 248 reverses a rake of freshly-mixed steel into the gloomy interior of the rough-rolling mill at Anshan works. Facing page: an XK2 Class 0-6-0T. Anshan's varied motive power roster includes five engines of this class, used in restricted areas of the works where the loading gauge prevents the use of larger locomotives. Their shape is familiar in many parts of the world as they are survivors from the 500 United States Army Transportation Corps 0-6-0Ts of World War II.

Left: YJ Class Industrial Prairie 2-6-2 No. 290 simmers gently amid the blast furnaces at Anshan Iron and Steel Works. Above: another of Anshan's XK2 Class 0-6-0Ts performs her regular duty on an upraised section of the network over which larger locomotives are forbidden. Built for service during World War II by H. K. Porter, the Vulcan Ironworks and the Davenport Locomotive Works, these engines have 162 x 24in cylinders, 4ft 6in diameter driving wheels, a boiler pressure of 210 lbs per square inch, a tractive effort of 21,600 lbs and weigh slightly less than fifty tons in full working order.

Left: one of Anshan Iron and Steel Works' fleet of SY Class Industrial Mikado 2-8-2s awaits minor repairs outside the plant's repair shop, while (below) a China Railways JF Class Mikado 2-8-2 receives a round of oil in the depot yard at Datong. This scene reveals the extremely handsome lines of the JF, her American ancestry fully evident. It was this kind of "Light Mike" that was prolific on so many of America's railroads three quarters of a century ago.

Above: the twice-weekly mixed train from Tabora to Mpanda in Tanzania heads gingerly along the lightly laid track behind No. 2611, a British-built Mikado which came from the Vulcan Foundry in 1952. Her traditional British shape is somewhat marred by the addition of a Giesl chimney, feed water heater, Westinghouse pump and air cylinders. She is the last survivor of the former Tanganyika Railway's ML Class and was specially retained for this line on account of her nine-and-three-quarter-tonne axle load. In addition to serving a Russian gold mine at Mpanda, this line is also important for the delivery of water to remote tribes during the dry season.

Africa is intricately laced with railways, and Cecil Rhodes's dream for a route from the Cape to Cairo could and should have become a reality long ago. Railway development in Africa was closely associated with Britain through her imperial, commercial and military activities. The exploits of British engineers, as they built railways across this dark and largely undiscovered continent, are among the great legends of the railway age. Indeed, railways opened up Africa as they did North America, although the difficulties of utilising and sustaining so alien a form of technology in an under-industrialised continent with many national boundaries and a proliferation of languages and cultures remains a problem to the present day.

The forging of railways on such a continent was a daunting task financially, so costs were kept to a minimum and from the outset narrow gauge lines were chosen and laid on track beds which were, of necessity, lightly laid with heavy curvature and steep gradients. This contrasted with the railways of the developed world that had been built to a larger gauge on firmer and more consistent foundations. Yet the limitations imposed by the narrow gauge were partly offset by the building of locomotives that were proportionally larger than those running on the standard gauge networks.

The continent's locomotives ranged over countless designs and wheel arrangements, many countries invariably going their own way in terms of design and policy. Until the 1920s many were conventional, British-styled designs, but the traditional 0-6-0s and 0-8-0s were unsuited to African conditions and instead often appeared in the form of 4-8-0s, 2-8-2s and 4-8-2s. As locomotives became larger, restrictions in axle weights, along with the tight curvatures, made the use of conventional locomotives increasingly difficult on many routes – until a design was conceived in Britain which was perfect for the African situation.

This revolutionary concept was H.W. Garratt's articulated design – the most important variation ever played on the conventional theme – which combined immense power with a light axle loading and the articulation required to negotiate the most tortuous curves. The Garratt's strength lay in the fact that the boiler was given its own separate frame and slung clear of all coupled wheels. Fuel and water were carried in separate units at either end, on which the boiler pivots were mounted. Thus, the double-jointed engine provided absolute freedom for the design of the boiler, firebox and ashpan, unimpeded by coupled wheels. The important question of weight distribution was solved by spreading the wheels either side of the boiler. Garratt persuaded the Manchester locomotive builder, Beyer Peacock, to adopt his principle and, from its inception in Edwardian Britain, it found favour in Africa.

The equipping of the Western world's railways with new forms of motive power and rolling stock created a whole range of industries keen to sell their products across all frontiers – and diesel salesmen regarded Africa as a rich hunting ground. The emotive appeal of investing in new technology is a great lure for Third World countries struggling to improve their lot. However, the use of sophisticated forms of motive power in the demanding conditions in Africa has often created problems, and many countries would have been far better served by relying on the steam locomotive's simplicity and longevity and concentrating such funds as were available upon improving track, rolling stock and communications, and investing in the right personnel.

Africa is no longer a haven for steam traction; gone are the red-liveried, fire-throwing, eucalyptus-burning Garratts that worked the famous Benguela Railway of Angola. Gone also are the world's last Atlantics from Mozambique, and gone now is South Africa – which until recently sported a few main lines on which the 25 NC Class 4-8-4s, one of the world's largest steam survivors, remained.

Neighbouring Zimbabwe's railways had the distinction of being almost entirely Garratt-operated, a unique situation in which several classes provided a variety of services, such as passenger trains being hauled by the racy 15 Class 4-6-4 + 4-6-4s. Zimbabwe's adequate reserves of coal and her capacity to maintain steam traction kept steam alive there well into the 1990s.

Another African country that wisely realises the value of steam traction is Sudan. Here, massive problems have been encountered in maintaining complex and temperamental fleets of diesels, so a policy of partial reversion to steam was begun during the 1980s, greatly aided by Hugh Phillips Engineering of South Wales, the company responsible for renovating many of Sudan's locomotives. These played an important part in helping to alleviate the recent Sudanese famines and, as such, the liaison work undertaken by Hugh Phillips represents one of the bright spots on the world railway scene. After all, it is surely obligatory for Western nations to provide such simple and cheap spare parts to the developing world, instead of forcing upon them a technology that is often irrelevant to their situation.

On the former East African Railways Corporation, which comprised the combined networks of Kenya, Tanzania and Uganda, steam has sunk to a low ebb, although several classes do see occasional use. Sadly, the magnificent 59 Class 4-8-2 + 2-8-4 250-tonne Garratts, which formerly plied the 332-mile-long haul from Mombassa on the Indian Ocean up to the Kenyan capital of Nairobi, have now been replaced by diesels, but most of the class still exists out of use.

Compared with Africa, the Middle East has relatively few railways, although Egypt sports a well-engineered network which was once a perfect mirror of British practice and performance. Today, with the exception of isolated examples in Jordan, only Syria retains a small steam fleet on its curious Levantine gauge of 3ft 3⅝in. Radiating from Damascus, two principal routes are in operation: one heads through the mountains to the Lebanese border, while the other heads due south and was part of the original pilgrim route to Mecca. Trains work as far as Dar'a on the Jordanian border, where 2-8-0s and 2-8-2s of German origin are active. Other types lie abandoned at Cadem works in Damascus.

The last working survivor of the former East African Railway's 25 Class 2-8-2 (left) performs shunting duties around the yard at Tabora. She was built in Lancashire by the Vulcan Foundry in 1926 and looks completely at home alongside a typical British semaphore. The most spectacular line in the whole of East Africa was the 332-mile drag from Mombassa on the Indian Ocean up to the Kenyan capital, Nairobi. For many years, this was worked by the magnificent Mountain Class 4-8-2+2-8-4 Garratts (above). Named after the highest mountains of East Africa, thirty-four of these oil-burning giants were delivered to Kenya from Beyer Peacock's Gorton works, Manchester, in 1955. Overleaf: a brace of 16A Class 2-8-2+2-8-2 Garratts head along the West Nicholson to Bulawayo line in Rhodesia. The wagon sandwiched between the two locomotives serves to achieve a more even weight distribution on the track.

Although steam traction has finished on South Africa Railway's main lines, some historic classes can still be found in colliery service. Left: a former mainline 4-8-2 heads from the colliery to the exchange sidings with a loaded train, the workers riding on the engine. These magnificent 4-8-2 tanks – along with a 4-8-4 variant – can be seen at many South African industrial locations. The New Largo colliery has two 4-8-2s and a 4-8-4, all built by North British of Glasgow during the 1950s. 4-8-2 tanks have been used in South Africa since the 19th century and these engines are essentially a modern update of the earlier designs. The first example was built in 1937, and they are capable of starting 400-tonne trains on a one in fifty gradient. Above: one of New Largo's 4-8-2Ts, decked in its superb chocolate livery, draws empties from the adjacent power station sidings.

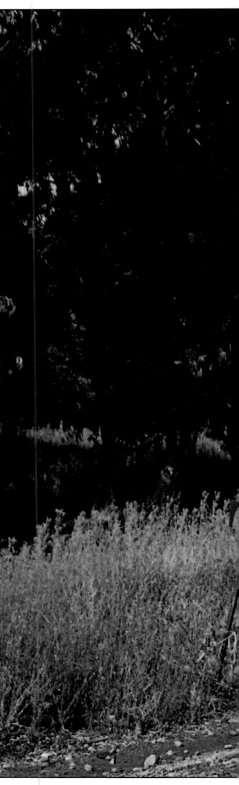

Left: the elegant Victorian lines of this ex South African Railways 7A Class 4-8-0 are clearly evidenced as she enjoys a further lease of life at the Whitbank Consolidated Coal Mine. She was built in 1886 at Sharp Stewart's Atlas Works, Glasgow, for the Cape Government Railway as a standard heavy freight design of the period. The practice of naming locomotives was adopted by various depots on South African Railways, especially at De Aar (bottom left), where many of the huge 25NC Class 4-8-4s took the names of their drivers' wives. Many hybridised locomotives exist on South Africa's industrial lines, the most common form being the 4-8-2Ts rebuilt into tender locomotives. These conversions are done locally, sometimes with bizarre results, but the example (below) at Tweefontein United Colliery in the Transvaal, has produced a colonial-looking 4-8-0. Many reasons are given for these conversions: leaking water from the tanks causing slipping, surging water in the tanks causing excess wear in the axle boxes, and even insufficient fuel-carrying capacity. In order to regain the lost adhesion, dummy splashes filled with cement or waste steel are set along the engine's running plate.

These pages: vintage steam operations along the route from Damascus to Lebanon. Friday is the Muslim day of rest, and special trains run to enable the inhabitants of Damascus to escape the searing heat of their traffic-choked city and spend a few hours of cool relief in the hills. The Lebanese civil war has long since prevented through workings on this line, and all trains terminate at Sergayah, on the Syrian side. Left: a Syrian 2-6-0T, built by SLM of Switzerland in 1894, prepares to return from Sergayah with an evening train to Damascus. Above: a heavily-laden Fridays-only excursion train climbs away from Damascus.

Above: a condensing 4-8-4 belonging to South African Railways races northwards through the Karroo Desert with an express freight. The fascinating, pear-shaped smokebox on these engines is designed to house the fan blower, which is driven by the exhaust steam in order to create the necessary draught in the smokebox. Notice the inordinately long tender, complete with air inlet meshing and also the slight leakage of steam from the condensing elements. Right: a South African Railways Class 15CA 4-8-2 storms away from Panpoort on the Pretoria to Witbank main line, having been looped to allow a westbound train to pass. Many important lines in South Africa are only single track, so passing loops occur every few miles. The 15CAs were known as "Big Bills" and, although of pure American design, this particular engine was one of a batch built by Breda of Milan in 1929.

The line southwards from Damascus was originally part of the pilgrim route to Mecca. Authorised by the Sultan of Turkey, building began in 1901, and seven laborious years later the line reached Medina, 809 miles to the south. But the Arabs, concerned that their Holy City would be defiled, refused to allow the railway any further and mounted frequent attacks on construction camps. Shortly afterwards, during World War I, sections of the line were destroyed by Lawrence of Arabia. Today, only the Syrian and part of the Jordanian sections remain operative. Facing page: a Hartmann-built 2-8-2 raises steam at Cadem depot in Damascus prior to taking a freight southwards to the Jordanian border. Above: the last survivor from a class of 2-8-0s provided by Hartmann of Chemnitz for the Hedjaz Railway heads the daily mixed along the pilgrim route from De Aar on the Jordanian border to Damascus and, returning later the same day (right), pauses to shunt at one of the many wayside stations.

STEAM IN SOUTH AMERICA

In common with Africa, South America is another vast region of the world comprised of countries which never built their own locomotives. Britain was the principal builder and supplier of railways to South America, not through Imperial rule, as had been the case in Africa, but through commercial and financial interests. South America's railways are among the most fascinating and varied on earth – here one experiences a multiplicity of countries and enormous geographical contrasts, ranging from the exotic trans-Andean routes, the jungles of the Amazon basin and the wilds of the Paraguayan Chaco to the fertile Argentinian pampas, the waterless deserts of Chile and the wildernesses of Patagonia.

South America is perhaps the last great steam hunting ground – just the place to discover an undocumented survivor. Modernisation has taken its toll, as have railway closures, which in some countries have been quite severe, but such isolated pockets as exist are eminently worthy of study. The exotica ranges from such delights as the world's last steam trams, American steam super power in the form of Texas type 2-10-4s, wood-burning Edwardian Moguls on the main line through Paraguay and the world's southernmost railway in Rio Gallegos, whose 2-10-2s haul 2,000-tonne coal trains.

At one time Argentina had the largest railway network on the continent – it is said the British built a greater mileage of railways there than they did at home. It was the British steam locomotive that opened up the vast, fertile pampas to become one of the bread baskets of the world, and in so doing, it made a significant contribution to one of South America's leading economies. British finance and engineering skills in this country were as predominant as they were in India and, not surprisingly, Argentina was the recipient of vast numbers of classic, homespun British locomotives, which for many years burnt coal imported from the Welsh valleys! Modernisations, closures and the general decline of railways has now ended this great chapter of railway history.

In neighbouring Brazil, steam survivors hail primarily from the United States. The country's best-loved system is the Dona Teresa Cristina, a metre-gauge coal-carrying railway in the south. This last haunt of the Texas 2-10-4s also operates 2-10-2s purchased from Argentina's Belgrano Railway. Brazil's sugar plantations in the Campos and Pernambuco areas retain a remarkable diversity of American, British and German motive power on metre-gauge networks, although many of the older designs are now out of use, joint victims of railway closures and dieselisation.

The situation in Paraguay is infinitely more exciting; here the world's last all-steam main line runs for 232 miles from the capital city of Asuncion to Encarnacion on the Argentinian border. Hardly anything has changed since the Edwardian engineers converted the line to standard gauge in 1910; some of the original Moguls remain operative, along with other British designs purchased in recent years from Argentina's Urquiza railway. The Paraguayan system, whose veteran wood-burning locomotives throw crimson embers a hundred feet into the air, is one of the highlights of the world steam scene. The workshops that maintain the system are set in the rural village of Sapucay and much of the machinery is steam powered, as was original nineteenth-century practice.

Uruguay has also been a major user of British Moguls since the early years of the century. The country's railways were financed and constructed by Britain and many of the engines came from Beyer Peacock's Gorton works. It seems likely that the Manchester connection with the Fray Bentos meat company was one of the reasons why that city provided so many of Uruguay's locomotives. The older Beyer Peacock survivors are the 2-6-0 tanks, some of which date back to the 1880s, but far more significant are the derelict examples of the world's last 4-4-4 suburban tanks. These graceful and beautifully proportioned machines are reminiscent of similar engines on the Wirral Railway and are the only surviving examples of this wheel arrangement – none exist in preservation. A massive investment in a road system has decimated Uruguay's railways and although isolated steam workings remain in several parts of the country, these are now confined to tripping and shunting duties.

Elsewhere, amid the vastness of South America, enclaves of steam traction survive, albeit often derelict, like the American classics dumped in the depot at Puerto Eten in Peru, such as a magnificent Rogers 4-4-0 complete with wooden cab – a definitive example of early American locomotive practice. Equally exotic rarities, like the last articulated Ritson Meyer 0-6-6-0s on the nitrate railways of Chile's Atacama Desert, have recently passed into history.

The magnificent British-built 4-8-0s were the principal freight haulers during the latter days of the Buenos Aires and Great Southern Railway. Facing page: one of a later batch delivered from the Vulcan Foundry in 1948, the year in which Argentina's railways were nationalised.

Argentina's former Buenos Aires and Great Southern Railway was almost entirely British financed, built and operated. It was one of the best-run railways in the world and its 5ft 6in inch gauge main lines opened up the fertile pampas and enabled the conveyance of inordinate tonnages of beef and grain to the Atlantic ports 'The BAGS', as the Railway was affectionately known, played a vital part in advancing Argentina's economy, making it one of the richest countries in the world. Such achievements are long since part of Argentina's history. Today, the unfashionableness of railways, combined with heavy dieselisation, has decimated former British designs. Facing page: a former BAGS 2-6-2T, built by Nasmyth Wilson at their Bridgewater foundry in Patricroft, Manchester, in 1907, eases a ballast train out of the sidings at Tandil. Above and right: a classic Scottish Pug in far flung Argentina, No. 2562 was the last survivor of a large class of 0-6-0 saddle tanks which formed a standard shunting design. She was built by Kerr Stuart of Stoke-upon-Trent in 1913, but the class originated from the North British of Glasgow in 1904 and bears all the hallmarks of a traditional Scottish 0-4-0 Pug developed during the middle years of the 19th century.

Top left: Argentina's metre-gauge Belgrano Railway Class 10A 2-6-2 No. 4606 heads away from Santa Fe with a pick-up freight. She was built by Société Suisse in 1909, during the time that the French owned the Santa Fe Railway. Earlier the same day, at the Sante Fe shed, No. 4606 (above) was summoned to cover for a failed diesel. Steam was raised hastily as heavy jets of oil were sprayed into the firebox. Soon her boiler pressure of 175 pounds was reached, and the seventy-year-old Swiss-built veteran was ready to tow the failed diesel back to the depot and take over the yard shunt. Left: a former Buenos Aires and Great Southern Railway 2-6-2 suburban tank ends its days as shed pilot at the Ingeniero White depot on the Atlantic coast. Introduced during the early years of the present century, these superb engines performed magnificently on the heavy suburban workings around Buenos Aires.

In the vastness of Brazil survive some of the world's most fascinating steam engines. The principal areas of steam activity are the sugar plantations of the Campos and, to a lesser extent, the Pernambuco regions further north. The diversity is indicated by the accompanying pictures, which show a British-built 4-4-0, 2-6-0 and 2-8-0. This lovely Mogul (bottom left) works for the Usina Santa Maria and is pictured far out in the plantations waiting for a rake of empty cane wagons to be filled. Notice her chimney top eaten away after years of fiery endeavour. She was one of a batch of Moguls delivered to the Leopoldina Railway from Beyer Peacock's works in Manchester during the 1890s. She was No. 204 and still bears the original plate on her cab side. Usina Santa Maria also sports this handsome 2-8-0 (left) which the Leopoldina Railway received from the North British of Glasgow in 1904. She is seen in the factory confines against piles of bagasse, which is used to fire the boilers of the mill. Below: one of Latin America's most delightful steam survivors is this handsome 4-4-0, which survives at Usina San Jose. As the works plate on her smokebox clearly reveals, she was built by Sharp Stuart's Atlas Works, Glasgow, in 1896.

Top left: a Uruguayan Railways B Class 2-6-0T built by Beyer Peacock in 1889 shunts the yards at Florida. She is coupled to a six-wheeled outside framed tender bearing Beyer Peacock plates. Left: the last survivor of Uruguayan Railways' T Class 2-8-0s, No. 139 'Ing Pedro Magnou', heads a mixed freight along the rickety, weed-strewn branch leading to the famous meat canning port of Fray Bentos, on the River Plate. The class once numbered eight locomotives, which were rebuilt in Uruguay from Hawthorn Leslie Moguls exported during the Edwardian period. Notice the brass nameplate, unusually situated on the side of the firebox. Above: the Dodo of the Atacama. The world's last surviving Kitson Meyer 0-6-6-0T heads a demolition train away from Taltal, on Chile's Pacific coast. The waterless Atacama Desert of Chile was the last refuge for the Kitson Meyer, which was an articulated predecessor of the more successful Garratt.

Above: the most modern engines on the Ferrocarril Presidente Carlos Antonio Lopez Railway in Paraguay are these Moguls, two of which were delivered from the Yorkshire Engine Company's Meadowhall works, Sheffield, in 1953. Shown is No. 152, *Asuncion*, with her nameplate set on the cab side. Right: *Don Carlos*, a 2-8-2 well tank, built by Manning Wardle of Leeds in 1916, at work on the Quebracho lines of the Paraguayan Chaco.

Facing page: a Baldwin 2-6-2 saddle tank, built in April 1927, and the work's pilot of Brazil's Centro Oeste (VFCO) Locomotive Works. Above: Usina São Jose's magnificent 4-4-0 Sharp Stewart of 1892 at a loading siding that connects with the Rio-to-Campos main line. The veteran will head her loaded train over this line *en route* for the mill. Overleaf: the amazing contours of the Baldwin 0-6-2ST at Mogi das Cruzes appear in fine relief against the glare of blast furnaces.

Left: No. 313, a Baldwin engine of 1940, emerging from the dank, sooty atmosphere of the narrowly confined tunnel at Sideropolis on the Rio Florita branch of the Teresa Cristina Railway. This engine was sub-shedded at Pinheirinho to work local mine traffic. Above: emitting some fine stack talk from her four cylinders, No. 204, one of Teresa Cristina's stud of 2-6-6-0 four-cylinder simple Baldwin Mallets, returns to the mines with empties.

BUILDING THE WORLD'S LAST STEAM LOCOMOTIVES

The survival of the steam age in China has attracted worldwide interest as American-inspired designs still roll from the production lines. After World War I, America supplied mainline Mikados to the South Manchuria Railway. The subsequent Japanese occupation of Manchuria saw many identical engines produced in Japanese works and under Japanese direction in Manchuria, and these were classified JF. Another prolifically built version was the JF6 Light Mikado, which was originally supplied by ALCO to Korea. These were also built in large numbers for the South Manchurian and Manchurian National Railways. These two classes form the basis for the exciting Mikado building in China today as, in the post-revolution years, the JF was used as the basis for creating the present-day JS, which is effectively a JF with a Russian-style boiler, while the JF6 was slightly modified to form the SY, China's standard industrial Mikado. China's most important American derivative is the QJ class Santa Fe 2-10-2, production of which finished in 1988. Though descended from the Soviet LV Class, the QJs bear many American influences due to US equipping of Russia's railroads during the earlier years of the century.

Until 1988, production of the QJ and JS took place in Datong works in Shanxi Province, while the pure American strain continued to emerge from Tangshan works in Hebei Province in the form of the SY.

Although these designs represent the ultimate in Chinese steam development, they are remarkably conservative and represent the type of locomotive prevalent on American railroads seventy years ago, both in terms of design and power. The QJ has a tractive effort of 63,340 pounds and has been built fundamentally unaltered for thirty years – the increase in train weights having been fulfilled by double heading, which has for many years been a common feature on many lines. This rigid adherence to the production of a standardized design has swelled the QJs to some 4,500 strong, but the Chinese calculate that one type so tried, tested and understood is preferable to the expense and complexity of building larger designs.

This avid standardization has ultimately contributed to steam's decline, as one of the problems facing the Chinese railway bureaux is the movement of vast tonnages of freight, especially coal, millions of tons of which lie on the ground waiting for transport to various parts of China or to docks for export. Diesels of considerably greater power than the QJs are available, and many bureaux are now opting for these as an expedient as much as for ideological reasons.

During recent years, attempts have been made to improve the QJ; modified and new designs have been prepared, incorporating a range of technical and mechanical improvements which in the light of modern practice could meaningfully be applied to increase both efficiency and power output. One of the aims was to increase the thermal efficiency – the latent amount of energy in the fuel which is actually harnessed to do useful work. A general figure for steam traction is around nine per cent, but during the early 1980s, the Chinese claimed to be aiming to achieve twenty per cent. However, this was a political ideal rather than one based on practical application. Little was achieved and many of the modifications never got beyond the drawing board, although the government's Policy Studies Group maintained that the ongoing use of steam would be beneficial to China on the basis that utilization of home resources such as coal and iron would reduce the country's dependence on oil and the need to import expensive technology. However, the days of rigid central government control in China seem over; the railway bureaux have far more autonomy and they have ceased to order Datong's products. In a similar vein, industrial complexes are now showing a preference for diesels, not necessarily for increased power, but to reduce air pollution and utilize manpower more productively. Tanshang still continues to produce SYs at the reduced rate of between one and two locomotives per week.

Witnessing the building of the world's last steam locomotives is a spine-tingling experience; inside the shaded portals of the steam testing sheds, the engines receive their first breath of animation as they glisten in their flamingo works undercoat. They've just come from the huge erecting shops alongside which lines of freshly painted wheels wait to be rolled beneath the giants. In Datong, it was possible to enter the erecting shop at six in the morning to find a naked frame over the pits, and during the course of the day watch it develop into a fully-fledged locomotive. I remember standing watching these activities with incredulity when my red-blooded Chinese guide turned to me and said – and I'll never forget his words – 'Our workers move like Charlie Chaplin did in your old movies'.

In the boiler shops stand twenty different shells in various stages of construction, fitfully lit by the flare of the welder's torch, for there is little heavy riveting done today, inner and outer fireboxes all part of the affray.

In the forges, stacks of steel ingots, freshly delivered from Anshan, wait to be melted down for the manufacture of detailed parts, and blackened men move purposefully amid the gloom, against the ground-shaking thumps of steam hammers. In the centre of the shop stands a hammer of gargantuan proportions, performing its hypnotic task and exploiting the malleability of a white-hot Anshan billet, which it gradually elongates and shapes to form an axle.

Facing page: the smiling face of a newly-built SY Class Mikado peeps from the steam-testing shed at Tangshan Locomotive Works. Decked in her flamingo undercoat, she is ready to begin steaming trials on the nearby main line.

In the castings, we watched the demonic activities of the carbon converter, fed with a mixture of limestone and scrap from an overhead bucket. When the bucket's bottom capsized to disgorge its contents, the meshing hung limply in the flames, resembling a giant sea squid from the depths of a remote ocean, while the converter responded with crackles, grunts and sprays of sparks before bursting into a cataclysmic fireball to declare that the steel was mixed to perfect constitution in readiness for the filling of the mighty cauldrons which would make sedate passage by overhead crane to fill the moulds lying on the sandy floor of the shop. These moulds had already been dried by flaming jets of coal gas manufactured on site. As the cauldrons moved into position, the moment of contact resulted in a spill of fire, after which the moulds lay cooling through twenty-four hours amid conditions which could have been seen in one of the early American works in the middle of the nineteenth century – but this was Datong works in China in the closing years of the twentieth. Once the moulds were broken, the pieces fell to the sandy floor; there now began many long stages of machining. We remember the engineering disciplines and tolerances which machine tools exerted on the age of steam, enabling it to accelerate the industrial revolution with such force that we still feel its tremors in today's hi-tech world. Every piece was machined to precision by workers practicing skills almost two centuries old, for this was the building of the world's last steam locomotives.

Left: a dramatic moment of contact as the moulds lying on the sandy floor of Tangshan casting shop receive their charge of liquid metal. The cauldron has been eased into place by an overhead crane – the flaming mould on the right has just received its charge. Below: a malleable steel ingot is gently lifted from the furnace by an overhead crane in the rough-rolling mill. It will be mechanically rolled, pounded and cut into the prescribed shapes. Bottom: moulds being conveyed by rail for filling at Tangshan Locomotive Works. Overleaf: the demonic activities of the carbon converter in the castings shop at Tangshan. The scene vividly recalls paintings from the early years of the Industrial Revolution that depicted the smut-covered, white-eyed men subservient to the might of the foundry.

Above: smouldering castings at the beginning of their cooling process at Tangshan, a scene that could have been witnessed at the works of American locomotive builders over a century ago. The moulds will remain cooling for twenty-four hours, after which the rough castings emerge. Left: the driving wheel of an SY Class Mikado about to begin many long stages of machining. Within a matter of weeks, this unlikely casting will be immaculately finished and spinning beneath a 125-ton locomotive. Facing page: in the casting shop at Datong Locomotive Works the sand moulds are dried by flaming jets of coal gas manufactured on site. Notice the carbon converter preparing the steel in the background and the banks of empty moulds on the left.

These pages: the boiler shop of Datong Locomotive Works during the building of JS Mikados. Inner and outer fireboxes contrast with boiler shells, all of which are illuminated or silhouetted by the welder's blinding flashes. Above: boilers nearing completion await transference to the nearby erecting shop for assembly. Above right: the ghostly pattens of the welder's torch reveal the stay holes and tube positions for an inner firebox. Welding the boilers (right) has long since replaced traditional heavy riveting and is claimed to be equally, if not more, durable.

Facing page: one of Datong's many women workers liberally applies the familiar flamingo undercoat to the finished casting of a driving wheel, one of the most dramatic of all castings. Above right: driving wheels, lying in the work's yard at Tangshan, having passed through their first process. They are of boxpox construction – as opposed to the traditional spoked variety – in accordance with latter-day American practice. Notice the smaller leading and trailing wheels in the background. Steel tyres will have to be shrunk onto these wheels, and they are revolved at high velocity (right) while being heated by flaming jets of coal gas in order that the heating should be entirely even in readiness for efficient shrinkage. After passing through the intricacies of the machine shop, where high-precision tools trim the axle bearings and big ends to precise tolerances, the wheels are conveyed to the erecting shop, where they are placed in Mikado formation in readiness for the completed locomotive to be lowered onto them.

Facing page: last minute attentions at Datong to the precision finish on a QJ cylinder block, and (above) the cylinder casting for a QJ Class 2-10-2 nears completion. The machining of the valve and cylinder linings must be very precise, and at Datong the American practice of casting the cylinder and half of the smokebox saddle in one unit is preferred.

Datong locomotive works (these pages), located in the north of Shanxi Province, on the border with Inner Mongolia, was the last major plant in the world to produce steam locomotives. Since it opened in 1959 it has produced over 4,000 QJs, in addition to various batches of JS Class engines. The works covers half a square mile and employs 8,000 people. Most of the workers live within the complex, which is essentially a separate community. Entering the huge erecting shop and watching the mighty components of the QJs falling into place was an unforgettable experience. It was the sight which, throughout its closing years, attracted people from all parts of the world, and the activities were made doubly exciting when one realised that these last steam giants would almost certainly still be at work in the 21st century.

Above: lines of freshly-painted wheels, with their steel tyres firmly shrunk into place, wait to be rolled beneath the giants in readiness for towing to the adjacent steam testing sheds. Having satisfactorily passed all its steam tests and undertaken its high speed runs on the nearby test track, QJ Class 2-10-2 No. 6979 (right) has had its flamingo works undercoat replaced by standard black livery and is ready to take its place on the world's most rapidly expanding railway network. Any embellishments and adornments will be supplied once the engine enters regular service from its home shed. Overleaf: a brace of QJs, glistening in their flamingo works undercoats, stand in light steam within Datong's gloomy steam testing shed. Each new engine is steam tested for several days, and during this time it will make several runs at high speed light engine along the adjacent test track.

TRAINS AT NIGHT

The end of a busy day heralds a new period of excitement. The rapid pace relaxes a little, but the underlying urgency and vitality remain. When the railway's shapes turn to silhouettes, its sounds become intensified – the rustle of a signal wire, the clonk of moving points, the rumbling of a porter's barrow, a whistle within the gloom or a burst of steam, all herald the new drama about to begin.

The endless stream of passenger trains eases as the night progresses, giving way to freights: trains bearing the fast perishables – fish, milk, meat, fruit and vegetables – along with mixed commodity trains bearing every conceivable type of produce. Next the long-distance mail and parcel trains, some very fast and seldom stopping, others rumbling into mainline platforms to be met with trolleys piled high with mailbags, and occupying the platform for a length of time which would have been inconceivable during the day. Deeper into the night, the sounds of heavy shunting, the harsh staccato bark of locomotives, the musical clank of wagons, the grinding of flanges on worn rails were all characteristics of the urban night. There was something deeply reassuring about the sounds emanating from the switching yards; if the railroad was at work, normality reigned and all was well with the world.

The acrid, pulsating forms of locomotives bathed in a fiery glow was unforgettable; swirling steam tinted with a thousand crimson tones issued in blissful contrast to wraiths of pure white steam billowing against black skies. The veil of night accentuated drama, and when a locomotive issued pungent rolls of billowing smoke and steam against the background of yard or station lights, it wove an endless tapestry of form and light beyond swirls of fire in the foreground.

On the footplate, the men became bathed in an incandescent glow; the elemental and primitive forces given off by the locomotive demand the discipline, cool nerves and carefully focused mind which stem from long apprenticeship in becoming masters of the Iron Horse.

The intensity and drama of a night departure can never be forgotten. As the seconds tick away, the engine becomes a mass of seething energy as, against the deafening roar and swirling steam, the driver watches for the winking green light which will allow him to proceed. The ring of a shovel as the fireman adds a round of coal to the white-hot fire as the locomotive's pent-up energy struggles for release. Suddenly, the safety valves lift, a mighty column of steam shoots skyward with a deafening roar, followed by the scream of injectors indicating that the fireman is adding water to the boiler. Now everything is communicated through signs, for no human voice can penetrate the tumult. Upon departure, the shriek of a chime whistle, matched by the deafening roar of steam from the cylinder cocks as the driver struggles momentarily with the regulator, precedes the first reverberating cough of exhaust as the engine inches forward, the steady blaze of the headlamp piercing the gloom ahead becoming animated with swirling steam. The rhythmic, throaty coughs are suddenly interrupted by a burst of slipping as the engine momentarily loses its feet; the wheels spin in an oily network as a shroud of crimson fire erupts from the chimney, matched by sprays of orange-tinted steam as the fireman applies the sanding valve to the spinning wheels. Finding its feet, the engine soon becomes lost in a roaring ball of smoke and steam, but now the safety valves have closed, their sound replaced by the heavy exhaust beats and the rumble of passing coaches.

On the trackside, the drama is unrelenting; the musical throb of an approaching train heightens one's sense of wonderment and anticipation. If the night is damp, the sounds will be intensified, and as the train approaches the blazing headlamp may well be outshone by the dancing fireglow illuminating the exhaust trail and casting its reflections along the roof of the coaches. Flaming coals bounce along the tracksides and crimson embers shoot skyward with incredibly velocity.

Such was the all-consuming magic of the steam train, which made our world a more wondrous place in which to live. Its disappearance has left us infinitely the poorer.

Above: as evening brings some relief after a hot day, a Baldwin 4-6-0 of 1912 backs gently onto a rake of wagons at São João del Rei, on Brazil's VFCO 2ft 6in gauge system. The VFCO rivals the Indian rural railroads in being one of the most exciting narrow-gauge operations left on earth. Overleaf: a fine contrast between British and American saddle tanks at Cosim Steel Works, near São Paulo, Brazil. Both are 5ft 6in gauge; on the left is a Baldwin 0-8-2 of 1896, while on the right is a lovely Sharp Stewart 0-4-0 built at the company's works in Springburn, Glasgow, in 1903.

Left: Baldwin 2ft 6in gauge 4-6-0 No. 43 at São João del Rei. Above: No. 1, a metre-gauge Baldwin 2-8-0 of 1894 trundles a heavy rake of sugar cane through the plantations during the early hours of the morning at Usina Barcelos, in Brazil's Campos Province. No. 1 originally worked for the Sorocabana Railway, but she has long since been pensioned off to sugar plantation service.

Left: an Alco 2-6-0 of the 1920s waiting for her train to be loaded at a remote siding during the early hours of the morning on the Ma Ao Sugar Central System on the Philippine island of Negros. She is typical of the battered, multi-hued relics which ran on this 3ft gauge system. The barrel on the front – which rightfully belongs to engine No. 2 – contains sand, which is manually sprayed onto the tracks ahead of the train to reduce slipping in bad weather. Above: two of the world's most incredible steam survivors at the Maaslud Exchange sidings of the Insular Lumber Company. On the left stands a 0-6-6-0 four-cylinder compound Mallet No. 7, which has just arrived with empties from the saw mill, and on the right rests three-truck, three-cylinder Shay No. 12, after bringing mahogany down from the cutting area.

Facing page: the Brazilians have a delightful habit of referring to steam locomotives as 'Maria Fumacas' which means 'Smoke Marys' – a name which seems to suit these American-built cane haulers to perfection. Here we see Usina Outeiro's No. 7, a Baldwin 2-8-0 which was delivered to the Leopoldina Railway in 1894. Above: Finnish Railways' TK3 Class 'Little Jumbo' 2-8-0 No. 1163 trips around Rovaniemi, on the Arctic Circle, during a blizzard. Notice the birch logs piled high in the tender. Right: far out in the cane fields at night, Ma Ao Sugar Central's No. 5 waits impatiently to depart for the mill with a loaded train, displaying a full head of steam and curling wisps of flaming bagasse. Overleaf: a Baldwin 0-4-0 saddle tank/tank, one of Cuba's most charming locomotives, built in January 1916 and working at the Carlos Manuel de Cespedes Sugar Mill in Camaguey Province. She is an oil burner, the fuel being carried in the improvised tank added to the engine's running plate, hence her curious designation of 0-4-0 ST/T.

Above: a JF Class carcass, which lay amid a number of condemned engines, including four S160s and China's last KD2 Class 2-8-0s, built in Belgium for the former Lung-Hai Railway, an east-west trunk route across Central China. It is a sad reminder that even in the steam stronghold of Manzhouli, deep in Inner Mongolia on the Chinese-Russian border, older types are rapidly being broken up in order to achieve complete standardization.

GRAVEYARDS AND SCRAPYARDS

A moribund locomotive exudes an atmosphere and presence which can be positively haunting. Lines of cold, inert engines waiting to be towed to breaker's yards are now a common sight across the world. Many will have little, if anything, mechanically wrong with them and this serves to make their situation even more poignant. Withdrawn locomotives can be found in three general locations. Firstly, there are those lying out of use at their depots, often standing alone or in small groups either at the back or at the side of the shed. Secondly, there are dumps of engines concentrated at a specific site – a 'graveyard' – usually well away from the sheds, and thirdly, there are examples actually inside scrapyards, where they are likely to remain for weeks, rather than months or years.

The distinction between a graveyard and scrapyard is enormous. In the former, the engines lie silently rusting, invariably accompanied by ever-encroaching vegetation. In tropical lands this can grow to enormous proportions as branches, trees and creepers liberally festoon the silent hulks. Wherever there is rusting metal, wild flowers seem to abound, and when these deck the engines in funereal purples, they provide a perfect background to the overriding mood of morbidity. Here the silence might be broken only by the soft, summery drone of bees – a dramatic contrast to the scrapyard, where the quiet humming of insects is replaced by the wrenching sounds of tearing metal and the bitter stench of acetylene gas. Breaking up a locomotive is a formidable task and one that is seldom done haphazardly. Even an example of modest size is worth a considerable sum of money, as there are many grades of metal, including non-ferrous items like copper fireboxes, which are always held at a premium.

The scrapyard is also a place of great flux; the piles of metal change almost daily, while in the graveyard, nothing changes, the shadows fall in predictable patterns, the plants and grasses flower and seed in their uninterrupted cycle and insects and birds proliferate.

The origin of a graveyard is often the consequence of indecision when, following the modernisation of a whole or part of a network, the locomotives are set aside, ostensibly as a reserve. Maybe they will be needed again one day in the event of a fuel crisis or a war? In other instances, it is a case of *manana* – a bureaucratic inability to agree a disposal price and method – and with scrap generally increasing in value, there is little incentive to reach speedy conclusions. In Scandinavia, Eastern Europe and Russia, some reserves are mothballed and the engines greased and boarded up, but these are exceptions – most of the world's dumps are left to go wild.

The ultimate dispatch of condemned locomotives takes many forms; sometimes they are cut up at the works of the owning railway and their parts cannibalised to keep other examples of the same type in service, or alternatively, they may be sold to contractors, who either come to the site and break the engines up or have them towed to their own yard. Where individual engines are concerned, the scrap contractor may well turn up with a lorry and several men and enact the job on the spot. A fascinating example of this occurred at a coalfield in Pathardi, Bengal, after a local scrapman had won the contract to break up a Beyer Peacock coalfield tank. He, along with eight of his men, turned up at the depot and pitched a tent in which they were all to live, and then they proceeded to demolish the hapless engine over the ensuing days with the aid of hammers! Where larger concentrations of engines are concerned, however, it is usually considered expedient to convey them to a scrapyard.

Some graveyards have achieved considerable fame; those in Greece, for example, were highly distinctive. Some of the sites were fifteen years old when they were finally closed and contained veterans ranging from Austro-Hungarian designs through to American types delivered as part of U.S aid to the allies during World War II.

In Britain, apart from closed depots which contained withdrawn engines pending ultimate disposal, the steam locomotive disappeared very quickly – but for the single exception of Woodham's yard in Barry, South Wales. This scrapyard, which eventually turned into a huge graveyard, originally took over 200 locomotives from British Railways during the early 1960s. Hardly any were broken up and their retention provided a vast repository for preservationists, who had time to build up funds to buy particular engines, having put a reserve on the items of their choice. Dozens of locomotives were subsequently rescued from Woodham's yard in this way, including many of those currently seen hauling specials over British Rail's main lines, and today, some thirty years after the first examples were consigned to Barry, the last handful are being rescued. This yard belies the glorious suggestion that hundreds of British locomotives have been stored in abandoned tunnels as part of a strategic reserve – a tale which occurs, with varying degrees of credibility, every few years.

Yet in the world at large, little basis for preservation exists and the half-forgotten lines of sad hulks which remain will eventually vanish into oblivion. Nevertheless, one can hope that a few unsung little workhorses now languishing in the undergrowth will one day be reclaimed by future generations as silent witnesses to the greatest of the railway's legends.

Until the early 1980s, Greece had six locomotive graveyards spread around the country, which between them contained more than a hundred locomotives. Most of the sites were at least fifteen years old and, in the case of the metre-gauge dumps on the Peloponnese, contained many nineteenth-century locomotives. Perhaps the most significant dump was the one at the old station in Thessalonika (these pages). In this amazing tapestry can be seen Austrian-designed 0-10-0s and 2-10-0s, S160 2-8-0s and Britain's first 2-10-0s of Austerity design built for service during World War II. It seemed that these locomotive mausoleums were going to last for ever until, without warning, the locomotives at all sites were sold to private scrap contractors who, within months, had obliterated this enormous chapter of Greek railway history.

Above: this scene in the breaker's yard at Sultanpur, in Northern India, during the mid 1970s shows the mass breaking up of former British types which took place during that period A line of inside cylinder 0-6-0s dating back to the BESA years is seen on the left, alongside a boiler from one of the XA Class light Pacifics from the X series standards of the 1920s and '30s. The cab side of the left-hand engine indicates that she was an SGS Class, whilst the LKO is an abbreviation for Lucknow, the engine's last home depot. She was built at Armstrong Whitworth's legendary works on the Scotswood Road in Newcastle-upon-Tyne in 1923. Right: a piston lies forlornly against pieces of abandoned anatomy on the floor of the breaker's yard.

Left: another scene at Sultanpur, as the boiler of an SGS Class inside cylinder 0-6-0 is cut open, revealing the tubes coloured white from scale. The dome cover has fallen to the ground, as has the lamp from the buffer beam, whilst the pile of flaming oil rags in the foreground is used to ignite the acetylene torch. Above: the wheel has come full circle for this mighty XE Class Mikado 2-8-2 built on the Clyde by William Beardmore of Dalmuir in 1930. For almost half a century these giants hauled 2,000-tonne coal trains over the hill regions of Bengal. They were the most powerful conventional locomotives to work on Indian Railways and a total of ninety-three were put into traffic between their inception in 1928 and 1945, when the final batch was delivered. The earlier BESA type 2-8-0 in the background emphasises the XE's mighty proportions. Notice the pieces of anatomy in the foreground: a piston, crank axle, dome cover, chimney, valves, springs, wheel fragments and a buffer.

Above: a tale of two engines. Sudan Railway's 500 Class No. 514 resembles the carcass of a dead animal as it lies alongside the Rabak to Knana line following a derailment many years ago. In the background, sister engine No. 541 approaches with a mixed train. The 500 Class are Sudan's most powerful freight locomotives and were delivered to the Sudan in the form of aid from the North British works of Glasgow during the 1950s. By 1983, when this picture was taken, a serious shortage of spare parts had led to only three members of the class remaining in service, despite the fact that they were needed and were preferable in Sudanese conditions to the temperamental and complex nature of diesel locomotives. The situation is a little better today, with Britain somewhat belatedly assisting with the supply of spares, both for the 500 Class and other types of locomotive in the Sudan. Right: the wreck of *Khor Doniya*, a Sudan Railways Pacific No. 245 built by North British, lies at the bottom of a bank on the lightly laid section between Sennar and Damazeen. The disaster occurred during a night of exceptionally heavy rain, which caused the embankment to give way. The engine is irretrievable and destined to lie in that remote spot for all time, as the Damazeen section is too lightly laid to permit a sufficiently heavy crane to facilitate a rescue.

Left: the atmosphere of the locomotive graveyard is epitomised in this scene from Cadem works, Damascus, showing the remains of a Hartmann-built 2-8-0 dating back to the early years of the present century. Above: the 0-4-2 was one of the earliest forms of passenger locomotive; it evolved during the 1830s and had all but vanished by the early decades of the 20th century. Accordingly, the discovery of this hulk in Java during the 1970s was of tremendous significance. Of typical Beyer Peacock design, she was delivered to Java during the 1880s for the island's standard-gauge network, although nothing had operated on this gauge since 1942, when the Japanese invaded Java and looted all the standard-gauge equipment for shipment to Manchuria. And so this amazing survivor was left abandoned in the jungle for the following thirty-five years.

Left: the Polish State Railways 600mm gauge PX27 Class 0-8-0T No. 775 lies abandoned near Wenecja. Above: the scene in the Feldbahn graveyard at Czarna Bialostocka, featuring Feldbahn TX Class No. 232 built by Henschel in 1916 for operations during World War I.

Above: the Insular Lumber Company's incredible 0-6-6-0 four-cylinder compound Mallet lies abandoned following the cessation of logging operations. The haunted atmosphere which always surrounded this engine during its chequered career remains in full evidence despite its moribund state. Right: this 0-4-2 side tank lying abandoned on the privately owned Rejo Agung sugar plantation in Java is one of the island's rarest locomotives. She came from the little-known Dickson Manufacturing Company of Scranton, Pennsylvania, whose last locomotive was turned out in 1909 and the example seen here is one of five which the company sent to Java in 1900.

Left: the wreck of *Tithorea*, one of the stately Austrian Class 580 2-10-0s which until the 1960s hauled heavy passenger trains over the main line from Athens to Thessalonika. Following an accident many years ago, this example was pushed into a line-side coppice and abandoned. Above: Britain's first 2-10-0s were built for military operations during World War II. All came from the North British of Glasgow and, in common with other designs for wartime, saw service over a wide area. Sixteen were ceded to Greece after the war, and these examples survived long after their sisters had vanished from other countries. Their light axle loading rendered them suitable for a wide variety of routes, particularly in the north, on the main line leading to the Turkish border. Classified Lb by the Greek State Railways, three of the class are depicted here in the locomotive graveyard at Thessalonika. Overleaf: another scene from the Thessalonika graveyard in northern Greece, depicting one of the Austrian 580 Class 2-10-0s. Classified La by the Greek State Railways, this engine was built for Greece in 1927 by Skoda of Czechoslovakia.

Above: the end of the steam age in Ghana as British built locomotives lie abandoned at Location works. Facing the camera is Hunslet 0-8-0T, flanked on the left by a Beyer Peacock Pacific, and on the right by a Vulcan Foundry 4-8-2. Right and above right: further examples of Britain's engineering prowess amid the locomotives and machine tools at Location works. The building of Ghana Railways over the uncharted, swamp-infested, malaria-riddled interior of the Gold Coast is a typical example of Britain's legendary pioneering of railways across the world. Overleaf: out to grass. The abandonment of railway operations on the sugar plantations around Tebicuary, in Paraguay, rendered these metre-gauge veterans redundant. An Orenstein and Koppel 0-4-0 well tank (left) reposes alongside *Baby Chaco*, an 0-6-0 of 1898 with Stephenson link motion.

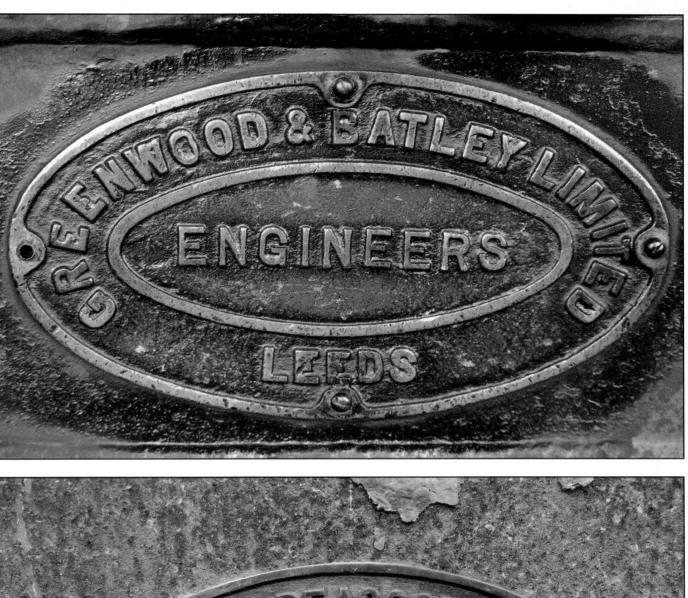

Left: a dumped S160 Class 2-8-0 for whom the wheel has come full circle, in Thessalonika in Northern Greece. Wherever there is rusting metal, wild flowers abound. Notice the flangeless driving wheel that gave these war veterans increased manoeuvrability on curves. Below left: a USATC 0-6-0T, another weary workhorse from the Second World War, lies abandoned at Thessalonika. She is No. 59, a Davenport engine of 1943, released from army service to the Greek State Railways in 1946. Below: the world's last giant Mallets ended their days amid the volcanic highlands of Java. These engines constituted an exciting example of American steam superpower, scaled down for 3ft 6in gauge operation, and are shown in the scrapyard of the Indonesian Railways' main locomotive works in Madiun. On the left is an Indonesian State Railways D52 Class 2-8-8-0, built in Europe, behind which lies one of the earlier DD51 2-8-8-0s, delivered from Alco in 1919. The works plate of the European Mallet, from Hartmann of Chemnitz, lies in the right foreground, while the Alco's number plate can be seen front left. Notice the lamp from a B53 Class 4-4-0.

Above: a Porter Mogul, long since abandoned, lies amid the undergrowth near the Guillermo Moncada Sugar Mill in Cuba's Cienfuegos Province. She is a 2ft 6in gauge engine of 1920 – Porter's familiar shield-shaped works plate is visible on the side of the smokebox saddle. Above right: a Baldwin 2-8-0, also of 1920, lies abandoned at Guillermo Moncada Mill. The tracks have long since been lifted and the engine was jacked up in order to cannibalize the axles and various other working parts to keep sister locomotives in service. Right: a Baldwin works' No. 57797 of 1924 is another sad hulk, also of 2ft 6in gauge, seen in the yard of the Rafael Freyre Mill in Cuba's Holguin Province. As the tender indicates, this engine was transferred from Paraguay Mill, but was found to be a poor steamer, unable to handle the necessary loads, so, after working for a few months at Rafael Freyre, she was abandoned.

One of the most celebrated Greek locomotive graveyards was situated near the village of Tithorea, on the Thessalonika-to-Athens main line. The dump here contained around forty locomotives, among which were a dozen S160s, including Greek Railways No. 573 (left), an Alco engine of October 1942 that lay in the far corner of the dump. Above: the haunted four-cylinder compound 0-6-6-0 Mallet No. 7 lies abandoned after the closure of the Insular Lumber Company's railroad on the Philippine island of Negros. So ended a great American tradition of steam and logging. By amazing coincidence, Insular Lumber's Mallet No. 7 and Shay No. 12, which enacted so many fiery dramas at the Maaslud Exchange, ended up side by side in the graveyard. This scene, and the one overleaf, makes a sad comparison with the one on page 267, in which No. 7 stands bathed in fire and spraying the tropical vegetation with flaming wisps of mahogany.

Above: a Schenectady-built Alco 2-8-0 of 1919 alongside 0-6-0T No. 134, formerly of the United Railways of Havana and built at Alco's Brooks works in December 1916, both found at Cuba's George Washington Mill. Notice the 2-8-0's wooden buffer beam. Right: the incredible shape of Insular Lumber's Mallet No. 7 looms out of the graveyard against a twilight sky. Overleaf: in her heyday, this lovely 4-4-0 worked elegant passenger trains over Brazil's metre-gauge Mogiana Railway and was one of a class exported to Brazil from Sharp Stewart's works in Glasgow during the 1890s.